Daily Self-Discipline: The Secret Road to Success

Do You Postpone Tasks? No More Unfinished Projects. Discover Cutting-Edge Strategies and Own Your Will Power, Even If you're Lazy AF

Table of Contents

INTRODUCTION 5

CHAPTER 1 – DITCH BAD HABITS NOW 10

    6 Surefire Ways to Quit Bad Habits... 10

    3 Essential Steps for Defeating Laziness 16

    How to Stop Procrastinating Now 18

    The 5 Rules of Self-Discipline.. 21

CHAPTER 2 – DEVELOP A SELF-DISCIPLINE MINDSET 24

    3 Habits That Build Self-Discipline.. 24

    4 Essential Practices to Ignite Strong Willpower....................... 27

    3 Techniques to Strengthen Your Self-Control.......................... 32

    5 Psychological Tricks to Boost Self-Discipline 36

CHAPTER 3 – THE SECRETS OF GOAL-SETTING 42

    How to Create SMART Goals for Better Output....................... 43

    How to Create HARD Goals for Higher Excellence 47

    The Secrets to Turning Your Goals into Achievable Steps 52

    How to Reward Yourself for Progress....................................... 55

    4 Ways to Create a Goal-Friendly Environment........................ 59

CHAPTER 4 - TECHNIQUES TO AMP UP OUTPUT 63

Transform Your Life with the Getting Things Done (GTD) Method .. 63

Achieve More with the Pomodoro Technique 68

4 Productive Habits of the Zen-to-Done Method.................................. 72

Using the "Don't Break the Chain" Technique for Consistency 76

4 Science-Backed Hacks for Increased Productivity 78

CHAPTER 5 - PLANNING FOR DAILY SUCCESS............................ 82

6 Morning Routines to Start the Day on Top.. 82

4 Evening Routines to End the Day Just Right.................................... 87

Eat These 3 Foods for a Productive Brain 93

15 Daily Affirmations to Teach Your Brain Self-Discipline............... 97

CHAPTER 6 - TOOLS FOR FUTURE SUCCESS............................. 101

5 Exercises to Test and Maintain Powerful Self-Discipline 101

How to Create Lasting Self-Awareness.. 104

3 Healthy Habits for Better Concentration 108

3 Unconventional Ways to Master Self-Discipline............................ 111

3 Transformative Ways to Push Yourself to the Next Level 114

CONCLUSION... 117

INTRODUCTION

Have you delayed your "big" project only to delude yourself you'll do it when you're ready — and that moment never comes? Have you fallen into a loop of laziness, and can't get anything done? Maybe you started working on your dream project, only to give up 2 to 3 days later? What if you tried to learn a new language like Spanish — but gave up after the first 2 lessons because the grammar was exhausting? Have you ever dreamed of learning to play the guitar, but once you actually sat through the lessons, the chords were too hard to learn and you dropped it halfway? We've all been there!

The secret to sticking to tasks you don't want to do is self-discipline. Everyone will tell you to develop self-discipline; but how do you actually develop atomic-level self-discipline that allows you to overcome each temptation in your daily life? The kind of self-discipline that allows you to create million-dollar projects, stick through daily tasks, and get s%*t done? The secret of atomic self-discipline is revealed in this book. You're in for a journey.

This book teaches you how to handle the hardest part of human nature: Biological impulses. Biological impulses work against you. All humans delude themselves that their thoughts are their own. However,, have you considered that your thoughts are not really your own? Look at what you do instead of what you think in your head: Have you ever thought that you should get fit and should be eating broccoli instead of pizza, but found yourself ordering pizza at midnight? This is not your fault, but the fault of your biological programming. Your biology is wired to respond to immediate pleasure: food, sex, sleep, entertainment. Biological impulses are powerful, and they cannot be overcome easily. Biological impulses run nature; if you observe nature at its purest form, all animals are essentially trying to consume energy or reproduce. The same biological impulses driving us and making life great can also destroy us. This is why self-discipline is key to overcoming our biological programming.

The 5 Grand Revelations of Self-Discipline

Revelation #1: You are your own worst enemy. There are no external forces controlling you, and no one stood in your way. You created all the obstacles yourself. Accept that all your procrastination, inadequacy, failed projects and unmet deadlines are a result of your own lack of self-discipline.

The first step to obtaining self-discipline is to accept you are in a struggle with yourself. Self-discipline is the art of overcoming your own biological impulses. Once a person gets through their main obstacle — biological impulses — they can beat all procrastination, lack of focus, and laziness.

Revelation #2: Human Evolution works against you. Millions of years of evolution have wired our bodies and brains to act in animalistic ways — your nature does not work in your best interest. Essentially, we're wired to take in the most value in exchange for the least amount of effort. To reverse our biological programming, we have to train our brain on reversing the process: We have to maximize output and minimize the value we seek in return.

Once a person's brain is re-wired to exert output rather than seeking the next thing to consume, their productivity goes up and this helps them achieve all their goals. The human body is not just a reflection of two parents having a child, it's also a continuation of millions of years of evolution which you have to struggle to undo. The brain is like a horse: If you let it steer on its own, it will lead you to the edge of a cliff. If you steer it right, it will lead you to your destination. This is why self-discipline is the key to overcoming our evolution and learning to use it to our advantage.

Revelation #3: It never gets easy. Self-discipline is a daily struggle, even after years of training yourself and rewiring your brain, you're going to struggle with discipline daily. This is because you can't detach from millions of years of evolution. Your body was wired to operate a certain way; you can only accept that you're in this for the long term. Reversing evolution is easier said than done, and it's a daily struggle. Even after years of self-discipline and exercise, people will still have a daily fight with themselves. But the main difference is that the fight becomes a lot easier.

Pro Tip: Results are produced in daily increments. Movies have conditioned us to expect a big motivational moment to hit us and, all of a sudden, we're supermen. But in reality, tasks get done with focus and momentum. Once a person rewires their brain to push through daily tasks, their work becomes a breeze.

Revelation #4: Self-discipline builds momentum. People go through loops of high motivation and high downtime/resistance to work. Both of those create momentum. If a person is trying to lose weight by jogging, the first few days might be hard, but once they've gone through the first 2 to 3 days, they build up momentum and it's a lot easier for them to run.

The same applies to work — once a person "warms up" at work by having a very productive day, they can repeat that behavior tomorrow. To be successful, you have to ride the waves of momentum. And once you start you have to create the moment. Each action creates momentum: If you're lazy, you will get momentum of laziness and never do anything. On the other hand, if you are productive, you create more productive momentum. This reflects on a much larger scale. For example, countries that get rich tend to get richer while developing countries tend stay in a loop of poverty.

Revelation #5: Your brain can be rewired for self-discipline. Each action "wires" your brain to accept that as a new habit — and this applies to bad habits and good habits. If a person starts smoking, their immune system will reject the nicotine temporarily. But after a while, the brain will wire-up to accept it and start craving the substance. This creates addiction in the person's brain because their brain is rewired to that of a smoker, even if they've never smoked a cigarette before in their lives.

The brain can also be rewired for good habits. Once the brain is forced to accept a new habit, it finds a million ways to accept it. Has your boss ever threatened that you'd be fired if you fail to complete a task on time? Under pressure, your brain can find a million ways to complete a task. Once you're forced to do something, your brain starts rewiring and allowing you to do the tasks you want. The brain can be rewired to get projects done on time, to focus on hard tasks, avert temptation, and perform at peak levels. This book will teach you to rewire your brain.

How to get Motivation to Start now?

Are you still holding off your life project? Do you feel you're not ready and do you want to start next year or five years from now? Starting now is the key to making it, like the Nike commercial "Just do it."

Life Hack: The key to overcoming all procrastination is a simple mind-shift: *"You're there when you do it."* Remember that phrase. There is no magical time in the future when you'll be "ready" to start a business, to have children, to stop procrastinating, to buy a house, to own Bitcoin, to do the hard tasks. However, once you actually do these simple things, you're immediately at the finish line! When you sell your first product, you're in business. When you go out and jog, you're successful in fitness.

The premise is that you don't have to lie to yourself by setting up an arbitrary future starting point when you can shift the date to right now. The only thing holding you back is your own permission. Give yourself permission to start now and you're already at the finish line. Achieving your goals is as simple as realizing you make it once you take the action, not when the time comes! Will you take action or wait?

CHAPTER 1 – Ditch Bad Habits Now

Are you struggling with smoking, pulling your hair, eating badly, or oversleeping? If your problems are simple and come down to one bad habit, you can solve it by rooting out that bad habit.

Habits are actions we do repetitively. Once a person repeats a certain action multiple times, it becomes a habit. Once a person repeats a habit for longer periods such as months or years, it becomes their identity. Many times, people can't remember what their life was like before they assumed their bad habits as part of their identity.

Habits can be good or bad. A good habit is to wake up early in the morning, or work hard at your job, to eat moderately, to meditate. A bad habit is to wake up late, consume substances you don't need, harm yourself, or engage in activities that deplete your quality of life.

To be effective in eliminating bad habits, we have to pull bad habits like weeds by grabbing the root and removing them from the ground up. We don't want to pull at the top of the weed, giving it an opportunity to regrow. All habits can be completely rooted out by changing your identity and rewarding yourself with each milestone. This chapter focuses on the shift in identity a person should make in order to quit bad habits.

6 Surefire Ways to Quit Bad Habits

1) Create a New Identity

To root out a bad habit, you have to do one important thing — create a new identity for yourself. If you don't create a new identity and you stick to your old identity, you'll be prone to relapsing and repeating the same mistakes. Smokers who want to quit almost never create a non-smoker identity; they imagine themselves as smokers who "gave up" smoking. They've smoked for years and associate every moment in life with smoking: coffee breaks, work breaks, friend gatherings, parties, travel, etc.

However, they have to tap into the part of their brain that remembers what it used to be like as a non-smoker; they need to go back to when they were younger as most people start smoking in their teens. Could you remember the time you didn't need a cigarette in the morning when you were only happy with a cup of coffee and you weren't tempted when you saw others smoking? That was way back when you didn't assume a smoker's identity. Now that you took the identity of a smoker, you find it hard to quit.

Bad habits are essentially rooted out by reversing the clock and going back to the time when you didn't do them. If you don't remember, then you need to create a new identity that separates you from your old identity that repeated these mistakes.

Bad habits destroy lives: Alcohol, gambling, smoking, drugs, bad food. People know what they're doing is not good for them, but that information is useless — the habit is too strong and they fall back in the same behavioral patterns. In order to not fall in repetitive behavior, they have to step back and create an ANTI-IDENTITY to their current identity. Anti-identity is a method to take your current identity and live by the opposite principles. If you're a smoker, take on the identity of a NON-SMOKER. If you're a gambler, take on the identity of an ANTI-GAMBLER. If you're an alcoholic, take on the identity of a SOBER person.

Pro Tip: You don't have to "hate" your previous habit. Many people create negative energy and hate against their previous habits to cope with their new identity. However, if you really assume your new anti-identity, you can "detach" from your previous habit completely and without emotional baggage. Even years after you quit your bad habit, you might still be tempted. But the difference is that you'll be tempted at the same level as a person who was never addicted to a bad habit. This means that you will be underwhelmed in your temptation.

2) Plan Future Actions

To create a new identity, you have to have a positive outlook on your future that will allow you to take the action necessary to quit bad habits. If you have a positive mindset, you are more likely to be successful. How do you get a positive mindset? Think of the positive benefits that will come from you ditching your bad habit. Think about what your daily life will look like.

Pro Tip: Think about what your daily life will look like and write your ideal day down on a piece of paper. Write down where you'd wake up, what you would do in the morning, how you would live. Create a visual image in your head for what your new life is supposed to look like.

There are benefits to visualizing your new identity: If you're a smoker, you will get many benefits from your future non-smoker identity. You'll breathe easier, you'll become healthier, your breath won't smell, you won't spend money on cigarettes, you won't be at the mercy of nicotine addiction, etc. The bad habits probably create more negatives in your life than positives; if you want you can make a chart and compare the positives of your bad habit (the emotional value it gives you) with the negatives. If the negatives outweigh the positives, ditch the habit.

3) Push Through Resistance

This is the hardest part of quitting a habit — the initial resistance. When you stop a bad habit such as substance addiction, your body will go into "withdrawal" and have you craving for the substance. This is when you're most vulnerable to relapse. People who quit for a while can maybe last a full week; but after four weeks or more, they might relapse because they're constantly tempted by external forces. For example, a smoker might see their friends smoking or a commercial of people enjoying cigarettes. They have to fight the resistance, which is the strongest the first month.

Once a person has dropped a habit for over a month, they can start to assume a new identity. The first month is the real test to your resistance and the temptation will be at its strongest. Expect it. If a person can go through a full month without a bad habit, they will likely create a new identity and sustain it for the rest of their lives. You must push through resistance, and remember that the negatives of your habit far outweigh the positives; this should be enough to keep you from repeating bad habits.

4) Replace Bad Habits

If you push through resistance, you're not done! You still have to replace a habit.

Pro Tip: People think its "willpower" that creates good habits, but good habits are created by replacing bad habits with new habits. Instead of giving your body your addiction, give it something else it doesn't crave. This will stimulate it the same, but the effect on your body won't be negative.

The best way to replace a bad habit is to create a replacement habit that will be good for the body. Many addictions are hard to shake off because they provide a high level of stimulus for the nerves and brain that make it impossible to quit. To replace those habits, you have to hit your body with equal stimulus but positive.

For example, many people who quit smoking say they did it with cold showers. Don't believe it? Cold showers that last three to five minutes in freezing cold can severely affect the nervous system to such a degree that the person feels literally no need for nicotine at all — the body has had its dose of stimulation.

Many drug addicts quit only by exercising or cold showering. This is easier said than done because a cold shower takes getting used to. You first have to smear water on your body by hand so you don't dive straight in the cold. Once you're used to it, you can go for small increments of cold. The cold will make you shiver, and it will shake up your entire nervous system. This helps with all substance addictions like nicotine, alcohol, even heroin.

Smaller bad habits like nail-biting and hair-twisting can be replaced by getting a squeezable ball that you scratch or play with instead. This will keep your hands away from your mouth and hair, and allow you to get your stimulation without harming your body.

5) Reward Yourself

Rewarding yourself is not a feel-good tactic; this is not something you do to celebrate but to re-wire your brain that the actions you're taking are good. If you're suffering all the time, if your addiction is eating you alive from the withdrawal, you must reward yourself incrementally in order to not burn out. Rewarding yourself is for the finish line: Once you've lasted a few days or a few weeks without a bad habit, it's time to give yourself a treat. You should endure suffering, and end it by treating yourself to something good.

Pro Tip: Treat yourself to a vacation if you gave up a bad habit. Book a flight to a new city or the beach, and spend a few days reminiscing at how good of a job you did. This will re-assert your new identity and keep you from slipping back into old habits.

If you suffer endlessly and you never reward yourself, you will burn out. You have to treat your brain like an animal; the horse only carries people and allows itself to be whipped because it expects a meal at the end of the day. If you promise yourself a treat after you go x amount of days without a bad habit, the reward mechanism will keep you going. This ties into a positive mindset.

6) Create a Milestone Action Plan

A long-term milestone plan is about sustaining your new identity. If you create new habits to replace your bad habits, you must keep them until the new-found identity is irreversible and part of your core being.

Planning for the long-term will allow you to create a new identity and sustain it. Think about your replacement habit: If you started with cold showers to quit an addiction, allocate a certain time of the night to repeat the cold showers. For example, your long-term strategy could be to shower at 10 PM every night: This is all you need in order to sustain your habit. The minute you make excuses or step off the habit, you will be prone to resistance and relapsing. Long-term resistance planning is all about finding a replacement habit and working on it constantly. If you achieve a 7-day milestone, give yourself a reward for that milestone. To be effective, you must assume you have a new anti-identity that is the opposite of your identity which created bad habits.

3 Essential Steps for Defeating Laziness

Do you have trouble getting out of bed in the morning for work? Do you struggle meeting deadlines of a project? Are you jobless and find it hard finding a job, or do you not feel like going to interviews at all? Laziness is a mental handicap; it can destroy your life because success is built on the opposite — work and productivity.

To stop being lazy, you have to change your mindset. Laziness cannot be treated at the surface level. If you take Adderall to focus or watch motivational videos, you're only going to last the few days or weeks until your supply runs out or you start feeling side-effects. Then your motivation will dip again, and you'll slip back to your old habits again. This is why you need a long-term identity change.

To solve laziness, you have to look at what causes it. This is an uglier side of laziness — you might be lazy because bad things have happened to you in the past. These past events/traumas or existential crisis may have created in you low self-esteem and a nihilistic mindset. Once you discover what your root cause is, you can work on eliminating it. Temporary fixes such as prescription pills will only last for a short time, and let's not even go into the negative aspects of prescription pills and other "focus" pharmaceuticals.

1) Identify the Cause of Laziness

To identify the root of your laziness; think about the history of when you started your bad habits — Did you get in a rut after you got fired from a job or you suffered from a break-up in a relationship? Did you move into a new city/country and had a hard time adjusting to the environment? How long have you been "sinking" in your bad habits? Think about the time before that, and what you used to be like. This will create a clear image for where you need to revert to. Simply take a week off to consider this, take a small trip out in nature and meditate on your behavior. You will realize where it went downhill and correct your bad habits. If you were always lazy, you will have to do the opposite — create a new identity to break the laziness.

Pro Tip: For most people, laziness is caused by a lack of mental clarity. Focus can be influenced by nutrition; food has a direct impact on the functioning of the brain. Bad food makes the brain unclear and this is why successful people overspend on good expensive foods.

2) Maximize Time in a Day

This is the most important step — not wasting time. Without realizing it, you're wasting five or maybe 10 hours of each day doing things that benefit you in no significant way. Worst of all, you might spend 10 hours a day doing nothing. How many times have you refreshed your Instagram feed today? How many times have you swiped on Tinder or talked to your colleagues when you should've been working? You might not realize this, but you've probably wasted a dozen hours you could've used productively.

To maximize time in a day, you have to shift your mindset from that of a consumer to that of a producer. A "consumer" mindset is about consuming external influences: social media, entertainment, movies, food, news, etc. A "producer" mindset is about output flowing out of you: making products, selling products, inventing, designing, creating, writing, editing. The producer mindset enables you to be at the root of life: You create the entertainment people are consuming, you create the social media content, you create the products they use, and you create the trends they follow. When you create value, people want to give you value in return. This is a key mind shift you have to make to be successful. Once you switch into a producer mindset, you'll appreciate your time a lot more.

3) Plan Productive Days

The way to do this is to act proactively. Your nutrition and bad habits could have a very negative effect on your focus and brain. High carbohydrate foods such as pasta, bread, pastries, and sugary drinks make your brain "clouded" and fuzzy. With these foods, it's almost impossible to focus. Your struggles might have come from the consumption of those foods. The worst part is that they're so widespread that the average person isn't even aware of how food can affect mental clarity. Meanwhile, foods such as broccoli, spinach, and steak reinforce your focus and simultaneously boost your mental clarity.

Once you've cleared your mind with good nutrition, you can plan out your daily routine. Start by waking up early and fixing your evening schedule. If you go to bed at midnight, you'll find it very hard to wake up at 6 AM. However, if you go to bed at 10 to 11 PM you'll find it a lot easier to wake up at 6 AM. You can plan your productive days by planning the nutrition you'll consume on those days, the time you'll wake up, the time you'll do your tasks and your work breaks. Once you've planned your days, it all comes down to execution.

How to Stop Procrastinating Now

Have you wasted years procrastinating on your "big" project? How about your job — do you delay work to the last second until the deadline is up, and then you rush it in an all-nighter? Do you have an idea for an invention but can't get yourself to start even after years of thinking about it? Procrastination is a disease that takes root in your brain and spreads like a cancer. Once it spreads to one cell, it spreads to your entire body and kills you. To eliminate the disease, you have to kill it at the start by not letting it take root.

1) Start Immediately

To stop procrastinating, you have to get in the flow immediately. Once your brain accepts that you've started working, it's going to find ways to keep you working. If you delay your project until the afternoon or evening, you'll probably delay it for the next day. This creates a never-ending loop of procrastination and you could waste entire months or years in this loop. Do you know of people who talk about one "business idea" or another but never do anything? They've been infected with the disease of procrastination.

All you have to do to stop procrastinating is to rewind the clock from a future "start point" to a current "start point." Do it right now! Drop everything you're doing — shut off your TV, tell your friends you're not going out, lock yourself in a room and START NOW. Don't delay this until the next day or the next week. Remember the phrase: "There is no better time to start than the present moment." You're prepared already and you must take action. Once you've started, you've done 90% of the work. The rest is all about building your momentum.

2) Optimize Your Time

The way you spend your time is unpredictable. You might think that you'll wake up in the morning and be productive, but turns out you only end up drinking coffee and watching YouTube videos until the afternoon. This is why you have to allocate key actions to exact time frames to optimize your time. If you take out a piece of paper and break down your day by the hour, you would be a lot more productive.

For example, you wake up at 6 AM, drink coffee, start work at 7 AM, work for 2 hours, take a 30-minute break at 9 AM, and continue working until 12 NN. Write this down on paper. Optimizing your time makes it impossible to fail because you'll devise a plan for every hour of the day. If you only tell yourself you'll get it done in the morning; you'll probably make up an excuse or do something else. Once your day is written in paper, you can actually execute based on that. Tell yourself that even if you don't finish your task in the time frame you allocated but you spent all that time working, that you still did a good job. Reward yourself every time you execute on your schedule.

3) Split Your Projects into Small Pieces

If you try to do everything at once, the projects will overwhelm you unless you split them in small pieces, which may mean spending a whole day working on a tiny part of a project. For example, if you have to write a 15-page business plan, start by writing 5 pages the first day, then write 5 pages the next day, and 5 pages the day after. In 3 days, you'll be done! This is much more realistic than forcing the whole project in 1 day.

If you load yourself on too much work, you'll find it harder to focus, and you'll lose motivation because you'll think you're not making progress. However, when you split your project into multiple pieces, you can check them off like a checklist. Reward yourself every time you complete a piece of a project by taking a break, or going for a walk. Eventually, you'll tackle entire projects by learning how to allocate them in smaller bits.

The 5 Rules of Self-Discipline

Self-discipline is about beating resistance, taking control of your emotions and doing what's right for the greater good. Self-discipline is not only practiced by Buddhists, martial artists, or athletes — it's also for the average person who wants to be successful. Self-discipline is an art form, and once a person understands what it consists of, they can start implementing it in their daily lives.

1) Self-Discipline Is a Sacrifice

To discipline yourself you have to sacrifice all your comforts and pleasures. You'll no longer be able to oversleep, overeat or indulge in negative habits. You have to sacrifice everything you knew as your "comfortable life." Self-discipline is not a getaway that you do for 1 week and then revert back to your life of comfort; it's a life-long task and the art of reshaping your identity.

To develop self-discipline, you'll have to go through literal hell and you'll encounter resistance on each step. Voices in your head will tempt you to go back to your bad habits — to procrastinate and not do what's right — but if you sacrifice long enough, you will learn to ignore them. This is why self-discipline essentially boils down to sacrifice.

2) Self-Discipline Is an Identity Change

Self-discipline is not about making your current life work. People think that there are "tricks" and "shortcuts" to keep their existing way of living without making radical changes on their identity and way of operating. If you're not prepared to fully change your life by changing your sleep schedule, nutrition habits, work habits and thought patterns, the chance you'll succeed with self-discipline is very little. Self-discipline is about changing your entire modus operandi, not making your current one work.

3) If You Know Why, You'll Know How

If you want self-discipline, ask yourself: Why do you want self-discipline? Is it to become a better person? Is it to do better at your job? Is it to quit a bad habit that impacts your health? Ask yourself: Why are you trying to achieve this? If you don't know the answer, you'll only be spinning your wheels like a hamster trapped in a cage and not getting anywhere. Once you know what you're trying to achieve, your brain will know that the sacrifice is worth it. Keep your end goal in mind every time you're tempted to sip back into your old habits.

4) Self-Discipline Has to Be Realistic

Be careful not to overwhelm yourself with unrealistic goals. If you work hard daily and expect to become a millionaire in one year, you might find that it's not going to happen. If you try to quit smoking and you quit cold turkey, you might want to start by smoking less the first few weeks and then letting go completely. In order to get the motivation to stick at a new habit, your brain requires proof that you can survive the change. Your brain doesn't care that you "think" you'll do it; it wants to experience the change firsthand. Do this, and your brain will give you the motivation to stick at a new habit. Start by taking small increments and then go radical, instead of ramping up on your changes from the beginning.

5) Doing What You Don't Want Produces Results

If you look back in life at all your hard tasks — the all-nighters you had to stay up to finish a project; the gym sessions that got you 6-pack abs; the hard jobs you did to make money — they probably all came from doing tasks that you didn't want to do. They were probably difficult to do. In essence, the hardest jobs and the things we want to do the least are the ones that produce the most results for us. If you can discipline yourself to focus exclusively on productive tasks and activities that increase your output, you can maximize your life quality and productivity.

CHAPTER 2 – Develop a Self-Discipline Mindset

Self-discipline is a skill, one that can be learned like riding a bike. Learn self-discipline as if you're trying to learn to ride a bike or swim in the ocean — it takes time to cultivate the skill. If you don't know how to swim, how do you start? You dip in the water and start practicing. Then you stay afloat for a while, and repeat until you can swim. You build the momentum to practice more until you're a swimmer. Self-discipline is based on 2 things: daily practice and momentum. To obtain self-discipline, a person has to hone their skills to build consistency and small-step their way until they've mastered the skill.

Why does a person need self-discipline? The answer: it helps you achieve difficult things like giving up your bad habits or performing better at your job. In order to achieve your goals, discipline is required. Self-discipline can be trained like any other habit; the key to success is perseverance. Once you strengthen your self-discipline, you'll be able to do things in life such as get rid of your bad habits, increase your productivity, and become fit and happy. Self-discipline is hard as it reshapes your mind to go beyond your basic emotional needs.

3 Habits That Build Self-Discipline

Pro Tip: To develop self-discipline, treat your brain as if you're an athlete and you need daily training to compete in the sport championship. What happens when an athlete misses their daily training? They fall out of shape. Give yourself time if you're just starting, and kick yourself in the butt when you're slacking.

The following are the #3 essential skills to develop a self-discipline mindset:

1) The "One Day to Success" Habit

The self-discipline mindset is managed on the macro: You have to prepare your brain for the long-term, but act in small daily increments. The #1 technique to obtain self-discipline what we call the "One day to success" habit:

- **The One Day to Success Habit: "If you did it for one day, treat yourself as if you're already successful."**

If you stick to your diet for one day, be as happy as if you've already lost weight. Don't wait until you have a shiny 6-pack to give yourself a pat on the back. Long-term success is built on small daily success and it makes sense to celebrate once you've gone through a full day of discipline. Measure your success based on what you've done in a day — if you've successfully disciplined yourself, treat yourself as if you already achieved your goal. Did you do your work today? If you completed your tasks, act as if you're already at the finish line.

This is a mind shift that will get your mind to build momentum by acting as if you made it once you've gone through a full day of self-discipline. Large successes are built on daily milestones. The wrong approach is to wait for 30 days or 6 months until you reward yourself and say you've made it. The right approach is to discipline yourself for a day and then pat yourself on the back for your accomplishments that day. Base your self-esteem and happiness on your daily tasks. If you did everything you needed to do for the day, consider yourself successful. If you failed, try again tomorrow.

2) Kill Instant Gratification

Human nature wires us to consume things that provide us immediate gratification: Bad foods, alcohol, cigarettes, the news, movies, social media — what do these all have in common? They provide instant emotional relief and gratification. Self-discipline is the art of optimizing your mind for delayed, long-term gratification. If you eat a candy bar that you know you're not supposed to eat, you'll be gratified instantly. If you say no to the candy and consume broccoli instead, you'll get a better body in 30 days. The difference is that you'll be gratified later. Discipline is different from self-control because in self-control we exercise restraint, while with self-discipline we essentially re-wire our brain for discipline for the long term.

Self-discipline is a life-long task that challenges our mind continually. Accept that as long as you're alive, your mind will always push you to take the way of instant gratification — that's your biology following a survival instinct. We always want to eat because back when we used to live in tribes, if we didn't eat, we'd die. We always want to have sex because if we didn't, we wouldn't reproduce. We are addicted to substances and social media because they ping our brain with dopamine chemicals that signal we're safe. The key is not to change our biology, but to observe it objectively and take control of it.

Pro Tip: Become God. Imagine yourself as God watching your room from above. To beat our biology, we have to observe our impulsive behaviors from a 3rd person perspective: Where are you at right now? You're in a room, you are reading a book. If you go to the kitchen, observe your behavior. Ask yourself: Is this person doing something rational, or are they acting primitive? Take control of your bad behavior by removing your identity from your actions, and looking at yourself through the prism of a neutral entity.

3) Create Momentum Waves

Once you've achieved your daily success, repeat the same process by pushing through your daily milestones. This will create "Momentum Waves" that you ride like a surfer catching a wave in the open ocean. Find a big wave and catch it. If you fall off, climb back on. If you exercise for 1 day, repeat your actions diligently for a week. This will create huge momentum for you to keep going for a full month. Once you've done it for a month, keep going for a full year.

Do you remember when you used to be at peak of your productivity at work, you kept producing on time, you were making money and your clients/boss were praising your work? You were in what's called a "momentum wave." Once you get the initial momentum, it's impossible to stop. Self-discipline creates momentum. If you push a rock down a mountain, the rock will start off slow but then the speed will accelerate. By the time the rock hits the ground it can be going at an upwards of 300 mph.

Once you start with daily self-discipline exercises, you will start slow, but persevere until the momentum builds and it will become natural for you to do the tasks that you previously deemed "hard." Essentially, we're in a battle with your biological wiring and minds on the daily. Once you realize there is no "permanent fix" (i.e. a solution that alleviates you of the daily struggle against your nature), and that this a life-long task, you learn to anticipate the daily challenge and create momentum gradually. Take it one day at a time.

4 Essential Practices to Ignite Strong Willpower

What do you do when you don't feel like doing something? How do you find the energy to go to the gym at night when you feel like sleeping and staying inside? How do you get up at 5 AM to go prepare for work when you want an extra hour of sleep? How do you get the motivation to do those things you're supposed to, and do them consistently? The answer is willpower. Willpower can be the deciding factor between a successful goal and a failed goal.

What is the difference between a millionaire CEO who runs his own company and a homeless person on the street? The difference is willpower. One has the willpower to push through and be successful, while the other one lacks willpower and can barely function in life. Some people want to be successful, and they know what it takes to be successful - but they lack the willpower to do it. This chapter focuses on the importance of willpower and top 4 techniques to develop willpower to push through your daily tasks.

Willpower is like a muscle in the brain. It becomes weak when left untrained. If you do nothing to practice your willpower, you will slack and be unproductive. Treat your brain as a vehicle and willpower as the motor: If you don't have a motor, or if you have a half-functioning motor, you won't be able to drive the vehicle. However, if the motor is well-oiled and the mechanics are functioning - you'll be able to drive your vehicle through the roughest terrain in the mountains. The same applies for your brain - when you have willpower, you have a functioning brain that will get you to do anything. Want to be able to wake up at 5 AM and feel great? Want to be able to exercise at night and look forward to your trip to the gym? Want to be able to work 10 hours without breaks or distractions? Fix your willpower – and you can achieve it.

Pro Tip: Treat willpower like a bicep. To increase muscle mass, you have to lift weights in areas that target the biceps. If you stop lifting weights, your muscles shrink. The same applies to willpower: You must put pressure on your brain to develop the willpower, but once you've developed it, the practice becomes easier. If you stop working on your willpower, you lose it and you fall off. Willpower requires constant discipline and daily sacrifice.

Willpower has to be built gradually - one doesn't develop willpower overnight. Be careful not to be too overwhelmed, even if the goals seem realistic. For example, if your goal is to exercise at 9 PM sharp every night, make sure that you don't burn yourself out too much or you might not be able to exercise tomorrow. Take breaks and reward yourself once every few days, in order to not burn out. Start by taking small increments, and build your willpower using the techniques below gradually. Once you gain momentum, continue doing it and the actions will become a part of your identity.

Remember the 6-month rule: What seemed hard for you to do today will become an average day for you in 6 months. If you thought running and lifting weights in one day is impossible, once you get yourself to do it once - you might find this is an average day for you after 6 months; and you'll add another activity on top. Your willpower will peak after your brain has evidence it's possible. To give it evidence, you must throw yourself in the line of fire every day. You will naturally have dips in the process, and you must pick yourself up. Once your momentum dips, force yourself to do it again and your willpower will peak.

1) Give Your Brain Proof, Not Promises

Remember this phrase: "**Your brain wants proof, not promises.**" Your brain works like a coin machine: Once it's given proof that something is possible, it gives willpower in return. If you tell yourself "I will eat better today", your brain won't notice and give you the willpower to do it. However, if you force yourself to do it - you cook healthy food and consume it; your brain will have definite proof that it's possible. Then, it will naturally provide you the willpower to repeat it the next day. Your brain is in constant demand for proof that you can do certain things, and you must feed it physical proof if you want to get the willpower in return. Have you tried quitting smoking? If you actually stopped smoking for 1 week, your brain would have all the proof it needs to give you the willpower to be a non-smoker forever. It's not enough to think positively and make reaffirmations that you'll do it one day. You must take physical action in order for your brain to supply you with the willpower you need.

Force yourself to do what's right for one day, and your willpower will increase dramatically. If you're back from vacation and lacking willpower to go back to work, force yourself to work immediately. You will work one day faced with resistance, but your brain will have proof that it's possible. Then your willpower will return and you'll be able to go back to work the same as you used to. If you haven't exercised in 2 years, and you've fallen out of shape, you can re-set your workout routine by going out at night. Find a jogging path, get dressed and start exercising. Once you've gone through your first night, your willpower to repeat the process will rise exponentially.

2) Start With Uncomfortable Tasks

What happens when you start work in the morning? You feel discomfort. What happens when you start jogging on the track? You feel discomfort. What happens when you go for a job interview? You feel discomfort. Discomfort is what you need; it means the action is worth pursuing. Now think about what happens when you push through discomfort - you become comfortable with the habit and you start engaging with it. The discomfort you're feeling in this case is not caused by lack of ideal circumstance — it's caused by your own biological resistance. Biological resistance tries to chain you in place and conserve energy, so you must do the opposite of what you're feeling inside your body.

Remember this: **Your body does not care about your goals**. Your body rewards you for doing things that actually stall your progress:

Sleeping, eating junk food, smoking, drinking, consuming media. Your biology is wired to get you to release the least amount of energy and consume as much energy as possible. Have you ever wondered why you want to do less at work, why you sleep late, why you want to stay in bed instead of hitting the gym? It's because the resistance is there to prevent you from releasing surplus energy that would actually get you to be successful in life.

Pro Tip: To be successful, do the reverse of what your biology wires you to do. Want to sleep? Get out of bed. Want to eat pizza? Cook broccoli instead. Want to stay inside and not exercise? Go out to the gym. Want to watch Netflix and slack off? Go work 10 hours straight without taking any breaks.

Tune in with your body, listen to what it craves biologically. In most cases you're doing things based on biological impulse, and if you engineer your actions to do the reverse of your impulses, you will create the willpower you need to be successful. Start with uncomfortable tasks, whether it's waking up earlier, doing a hard project at work that you've delayed, or going to the gym. This way the uncomfortable becomes the norm and you never fall prey to your biological impulses.

3) Give 100% Effort in Every Task

Willpower is not only about starting - it's about finishing your tasks at 100% diligence. How do you develop the willpower to do a task, if not by giving your best? The wrong approach is to start an uncomfortable task and slack through, thinking that by delaying the task you can still get it done another day. The right approach is to work as if your life depends on it.

Imagine someone put a gun to your head and told you, "Go out to the gym and do 150 pushups, lift 5 reps and run 10 miles." Would you find the willpower to do it? You definitely would, as your life is under threat. Treat your regular work tasks as if your life depends on your performance, and give your best performance even if the task is unimportant. Once you get used to doing everything at 100% capacity, it leaks into other areas of your life and your willpower to do many things at once skyrockets. You'll develop the willpower to work, exercise, date and engage in fun projects without running out of energy.

4) Cut Off Distractions

Remove all distractions that restrain you from completing your work. Once you've gone through an hour or two of work, you'll feel tempted to take a break and indulge in "relaxation" periods. The downside to this is that it's usually more distractions that arise once you discover one distraction. If you're scrolling on Instagram, you'll find your ex posting something that makes you emotional or an ad that encourages you to travel to Bali. You're suddenly on a booking page searching for flights to Bali - one distraction leads to another until you've completely lost track of your original work. To avoid this, treat everything as if it has a "snowball" effect that can potentially erode your attention and harm your focus just by looking at one thing. Remember how you develop momentum in willpower? The bad side is that you can also develop momentum in distractions, so watch that you're on the right end of that spectrum.

3 Techniques to Strengthen Your Self-Control

Self-control is about controlling your emotional impulses. Look back at your impulsive decisions. Do you eat pizza at 11 PM and wonder why you did it? Do you start smoking at a party and you've been trying to quit? Do you order something on eBay when you know you should be conserving money? This is what's known as impulsive behavior. To obtain self-control over impulsive behavior, you must take control of your emotions. Most emotions that cause impulsive decisions are hard to control as they're driven by anxiety, fear, stress or even happiness. Once you're feeling high on an emotion, it's hard to make rational decisions.

Pro Tip: Self-control is a *preventive* measure. One must observe their behavior to take control of their impulsiveness. Self-control is essential and impervious to making big changes in life, as the daily struggle of self-discipline is tied to making small self-control decisions of restraint. How do you last a full day on a diet, when so many food choices are available? How do focus on work for 10 hours, when you're distracted by social media? How do stop a habit that harms you, when it provides you with good emotions? The answer is simple - overcome your impulsive behavior. There are techniques to overcome your impulsiveness, by observing your behavior and correcting it before it takes over your logical senses.

Self-control is about to averting impulsive behavior. There are 3 steps to avert impulsive behavior:

1) Identify Your Triggers

Impulsive behavior is caused by a lack of logical judgment. When you think rationally, you know what's bad and good for you. Human nature is often more powerful than the rational mind and this is why it's so hard to overcome. The struggle of overcoming nature is tied to our biology, as we've evolved to seek instant gratification. Essentially, most things that feel good are bad for us in the long run. Impulsive behavior can only be corrected on the logical level, by making your rational mind more powerful than your physical urges. How do you achieve this? Start by applying logic. Identify your triggers in advance and act preemptively — avoid putting yourself in a situation where you're tempted.

For example, if you're trying to quit smoking, you might find that partying and getting drunk makes you want to smoke more. Avoid parties — that's your trigger. If you want to eat clean, don't pass by bakeries or other food stores that tempt you to buy food. If you eat at night, get a healthy meal in advance or go to bed early. Identify your little "triggers," the small events that cause your impulsive behavior, and prevent them by completely cutting down on them. Many times, you're exposing yourself to the wrong influences, by consuming media online that serves as launch-ground for bad behavior. Humans are influenced on a subconscious level too; if one sees their friends doing something on social media their brain tempts them to repeat their behavior. Cut of all influences that trigger impulsive behavior.

If the fault of the trigger is on yourself and you can't avoid external stimulus (it's not parties or stores tempting you but your own behavior) the solution is simple: suppress your emotions. Most urges disappear within 10 minutes. If you want to have a smoke, wait it out and occupy yourself with another activity. You only have to observe your desire to smoke, and surpass your emotions. Ideally you should avoid all external triggers and suppress your inner emotions to completely avoid sipping back into impulsive behavior.

2) Restrain Impulsive Behavior

Impulsive behavior is temporary. Taking control of impulsive behavior is essential to self-control as it signifies you dominating over your primal urges. There are two ways to control impulsive behavior: 1) Let it pass 2) Engage in another activity.

Observing your impulsiveness in the 3rd person can give you insight about how you operate and the way to suppress your urges. If you can remove your identity from the equation and look at yourself as if you're neutral person - would you still feel the same urges? Feel the urge as if you're 100% there and present with it, without resisting it. In meditation this practice is known as "becoming present to the moment." This will set your mind at rest because you'll know that your addictions and impulsiveness are nothing more than the result of biological impulses flaring up. The mind attaches personal stories to your impulsiveness, but in essence, it is a behavior driven by the brain's need for fast gratification.

Utilizing replacement activities is an effective way to control impulsive behavior: Go for a shower, take a walk, have a nap, go jogging, buy a boxing bag to punch, talk to someone, etc. There are many ways to regain emotions that you seek from your addiction or impulsiveness in a manner that doesn't harm you.

3) Prevent Future Relapse

Why quit smoking if you're going to relapse after 1 month? Why eat organic food if you're reverting back to junk food a month from now? Relapse is your biggest long-term threat, so knowing how to anticipate relapse is as essential as identifying your triggers. The way you control your behavior will shape your destiny, and anticipating future relapse can help you from sipping back into bad habits.

The way to prevent relapse is simple - change your identity. Many people mistakenly hold on to their old identity and try to "make it work" by changing their habits. However, the only way to succeed in long-term change is to change who you are as a person. You must let go of your current identity and become something else, similar to a caterpillar shaping into a butterfly. For example, if you want to quit smoking you can use techniques to avoid buying cigarettes and going to the store or visiting parties. You can even tell yourself that it's bad for you mentally and that it's a terrible habit. However, the right approach is to assume a non-smokers identity. Do you have friends who don't smoke at all? Do they ever feel tempted by smokes? The answer is no. This is because their identity is fundamentally that of non-smokers. Assume the identity of a person you want to become, and you will lose your current temptations naturally.

5 Psychological Tricks to Boost Self-Discipline

To build on your self-discipline and self-control, psychology can add a layer of willpower that will help you power through the hardest days when you're pushed to the limits of your emotional capacity. What happens when you burst through a week of successful self-discipline, and then you hit a breaking point and relapse on bad habits? The way to avoid that is to apply psychological building blocks — little techniques that when stacked on top of each other, can serve as a foundation for your psychological health. Think of psychological building blocks as bricks. If you had no self-discipline in the past, you can start building your structure by making it for one day. Once you've made it past a day, you can add one more brick. At the end you'll have a whole house.

Remember the phrase: "**The mind is a creature of habit.**" Once your mind is trained to do something, it can also be un-trained. If you've fallen into bad habits, you can reverse the damage by creating entirely new habits. This is because the brain is not definite and can be altered to your ideal form, in order to take back control over your life. Self-discipline is about taking control of the mind, and psychology specializes in studying the mind.

Psychological tricks are not about going to the crazy scientist that lives next door and have them hook you on electrodes that change your mind. Instead, you need to realize that changes can be made gradually. You once didn't drink alcohol — you taught yourself how to do it. You didn't even drink coffee — now, you can't go a day without 2 cups of coffee. The mind is very flexible and can adapt to harmful habits - the same as it can adapt to new "hard" habits which you're trying to enforce that would improve your life. If you have little power over the rational mind, the following psychological tricks can help you take control now:

1) Become Present With Meditation

How do you avoid bad thoughts that lead you to impulsive behavior? The answer is to not have any thoughts at all. Meditation is the art of becoming present and dropping the conscious mind, effectively trusting that your subconscious will be enough to help you make the right decisions. Our minds are preoccupied with thoughts about the future and the past. We spend too much time thinking and little time acting.

Meditation is an exercise that helps us minimize our thoughts, and the exercise of meditation is about focusing on the breath and not thinking for 20 minutes. To visualize presence, imagine yourself in the Caveman days - you were hunting an animal, you had a spear and the animal ran from you. Once you started running towards the animal and chasing for the kill, you don't think at all but your focus was on the kill. You were completely immersed in the present moment, which is what meditation helps to achieve.

The practice of meditation can reduce anxiety, make you more confident, and give you the ability to calibrate in the moment. If you're working in a real-time environment where you have to make decisions in the moment such as the stock market or live sales, you must be present to the moment. If you're stuck in your head, your thoughts will take over and you won't be able to engage with your work.

Meditation only takes 15-20 minutes a night and all one needs is an alarm clock. Set the alarm clock to 15 minutes, sit down, close your eyes and focus on your breath. You will feel the presence sipping in within 5 minutes, and 15 minutes out, you'll feel complete presence. Once a person has meditated for months, they can naturally invoke this feeling.

2) Shift Your Prefrontal Cortex

The prefrontal cortex is a part of the brain located above the eyes responsible for controlling focus. The prefrontal cortex controls focus by identifying focus points for the brain and using the senses. Once the pre-frontal cortex is "focused" on something, it can keep the focus for a very long time. You might think it's your brain that does the focusing, but it's actually a tiny bit of the brain located at the very tip that controls your focus and you can optimize it.

The pre-frontal cortex is an evolutionary reaction to humans living in the wild, when a wild creature could attack and eat you. In response, the prefrontal cortex immediately focused on the threat and made us aware we're in immediate danger. It also helped us hunt and reproduce. The prefrontal cortex has largely remained the same, but now people are trying to alter it in order to optimize their focus at work. Even popular focus drugs such as Adderall work by alternating the prefrontal cortex.

The fastest way to shift the prefrontal cortex is to force your brain to do a hard task. If you start the activity, the prefrontal cortex finds ways to maintain it. It doesn't automatically activate when you want it, but you have to force it to activate. Want to go running but your brain won't do it? Go out and start running, and your prefrontal cortex will give you the focus to finish the exercise. Want to work on your big project? Start doing it and your prefrontal cortex will supply you with the focus and energy you need.

3) Love the Process

If you learn to love the process that gets you success, you will automatically get success. Many people are results-oriented and try to fast-forward to the end point instead of focusing on the daily process that gets them the success. This is because we live in an age of social media where people flash cars, travel destinations, and champagne. As a result, people believe that success is only about the end point and not the journey. Understand that the tiniest action you take today will have repercussions 30 days later. If you step out of your house to go to the gym, you won't see any results tomorrow but you will in 30 days later in the mirror.

Watch your steps on the way to the gym and praise yourself because you're already successful. Those tired slow steps that you take in the night, that's real success. You have to scale down your process and optimize your behavior for the small tasks that produce results. The process is essentially a set of daily milestones that you do that produce results when compounded. If you put in 30 minutes at the gym every night, you'll be fit in 1-2 months. If you work 10 hour shifts every day, you'll be successful at work. Making the tiny psychological shift that each daily action matters and contributes to the big picture will help you push through the last bit of resistance you have.

4) Optimize for Delayed Gratification

Delayed gratification is about a long-term perspective. Success may take years. This is why one must prepare for long-term thinking and the sacrifices that follow. Gary Vaynerchuk, one of the leading media marketing CEOs spent a decade locked inside a room recording wine videos for his business. He didn't go out to parties or meetups. He honed his skill and knew that if he kept at it, his success would come even if it took 10 years of non-stop work.

A scientific experiment from the 70s targeting little children called the "Marshmallow Experiment" displays this. Children were given a marshmallow candy in front of them. If they ate it immediately, they only had that one, and if they waited longer, they were given two. Many children ate the candy right away while some waited and ate two candies. Later psychologists found that children who waited to eat two candies used to display higher problem-solving capability and had much better SAT scores.

5) De-Stress Periodically

De-stressing is the final follow-up to a successful work routine. One must take the time off to remove harmful toxins and reboot by taking the appropriate time off. If you're overworked, you're under constant stress and your body is filled with a stress chemical called cortisol. Cortisol is an evolutionary chemical that is responsible for external threats - if an animal attacks you, the body pumps you full of cortisol to put you on "alert" and make you more sensitive to the world. This makes you more likely to save your life when you're running away or trying to fight off an enemy (in an evolutionary sense).

The body can't differentiate between the modern world and the Caveman days, whereas if you're under constant stress from work it fails to recognize that you're in an office tower in New Jersey, and it pumps you full of that same chemical as if you were running away from a tiger. The effective way to de-stress is to completely remove yourself from your current environment. Book a flight to a beach, camp outdoors, go on a road trip, explore your city — do anything that doesn't revolve around your current environment. Once you de-stress, you can return to work recharged.

CHAPTER 3 – The Secrets of Goal-Setting

Have you ever looked in the mirror at your extra pounds and though "I should lose weight" but never took concrete action? Maybe you took action but give up after 2-4 weeks and reverted back to your old habits? Do you dream of quitting your soul-crushing 9-5 but never do it because you're too afraid of your boss? Are you stuck in a rut and see your life going nowhere? Is there an ambitious business idea lingering on your mind, but you delayed taking action for months or years? Most people think they should do it and they know they should take action. however, their daily routine prevents them from taking right action.

Goal-setting is about one thing: **Breaking your daily routine.**

The subconscious mind knows that if you take action, your life will change and it prevents you from doing so in order to chain you to your current regimen. You're a slave to a biological impulse. Your brain wants you to remain the same — this is a protective mechanism because it finds comfort in the familiar. Quitting your job, losing weight, starting a business — that's all unfamiliar so your mind will think of every excuse and rationalization in the book to keep you from changing. This is why you must set SMART goals that are time-sensitive and break your routine to get you to do what you need to do. Re-shaping your life begins at the goal-setting stage. If you set concrete goals, you'll be able to break your routine and start living the life you always wanted, one step at a time.

Start Now: "One Day" Never Comes

Remember the phrase: **"One day never comes."** You're only there when you take action. Have you held off your "big plans" for an imaginary date when you'll be ready? Are there ideas from 5 years ago that you haven't taken action on, but you told yourself you'll do them once you feel ready? Do you have a genius business idea that you never took action on because it's too complex? SMART goals exist to give you that last "push" that you need to kick yourself in the butt and take action. SMART goals are about breaking your routine and taking huge action towards your future goals. This chapter focuses on the goal-setting mindset that will push you directly into taking action.

How to Create SMART Goals for Better Output

Pro Tip: Goal-setting is like jumping into a pool. If you don't jump in immediately, you'll be tempted to stay on the sidelines where you don't get wet. If you actually jump in, you'll find the water is not too cold and you get used to the temperature fast. The same applies for SMART goals — you can take action immediately and complete the missing pieces on the way. You will never be ready until you take action, but once you take action, your brain will find ways to keep you moving. For example, if you quit your job with an abusive boss, you will start looking for a new job immediately and eventually land a better job.

SMART goals are the action plans you plan out before you take action. There is a distinction between SMART and HARD goals: SMART goals are incremental monthly small goals a person can achieve in a short time frame, while HARD goals are more long-term oriented and require deep-level identity change. S.M.A.R.T stands for:

→ **S-PECIFIC**

→ **M-EASURABLE**

→ **A-TTAINABLE**

→ **R-ELEVANT**

→ **T-IMELY**

SMART goals separate empty promises such as "I need to lose weight" and concrete action-plans such as "I need to lose 50 pounds in 2 months." If you set concrete goals that have action-plans and deadlines, you'll be able to achieve them categorically instead of dabbling and hoping you get motivation by instinct. If you lack motivation, SMART goals set the foundation for change by taking daily small actions. SMART goals have to contain all of the following:

1) Specific

SMART goals must be specific. The technique of is to write concrete dates and times that you can follow-through by taking action. When you write down your goal, start by writing specifics: date, time, outcome, and any other details. The more specific you are the more concrete you can be about your action taking. If you want to lose weight, write how many pounds and how many weeks/months. If you want to get a raise, write by which month and by what percent of the salary. If you want to start a business, write by what date and how many dollar sales you want to make per month. If you want to quit smoking, write when you'll have your last smoke and what you plan to do afterwards.

A Harvard Business School professor once tasked his students to write down their life goals on a piece of paper. The students quickly returned their papers to the professor. The professor read every single piece of paper and disposed them into the trash in front of the class — except one. He took the last remaining paper and read it out loud; the paper said: "I want to get a 10% raise by September of next year." He singled that out as the best paper of the class because it set a concrete action plan and deadline – instead of vaguely claiming "I want to get promoted" the student claimed that she wanted "A 10% raise by September of next year." The single difference in specific goal and time is what differentiates a failed goal from a SMART goal!

2) Measurable

Remember the phrase: "**What gets measured gets managed.**" Goals can be measured in the same way we measure our living expenses. Do you know what your rent is at the end of each month, how much your bills are and how much you owe in taxes? Think of your goals as measurable units. If you want to be successful, measure the exact increase in money you need in order to finance your future life. Let's say "success" for you entails a house. an average house in the United States in somewhere in the range of $250,000. What would it take for you to obtain $250,000? Maybe you want to start a new business to obtain that money, or get a high-paying job. Whichever it is, what gets measured gets accomplished in advance.

You can measure your fitness progress the same - if you had abs at 16% body fat, you can measure how many pounds you need to lose to fall to that level of body fat. Once you have a general measurement, you can break down your goal into small daily measurements. For instance, if your goal is to lose 20 pounds in a month, your aim should be to lose 1 pound a day. Measure your weight every day to reassure that you're losing 1 pound a day, and this will reinforce your long-term goal.

3) Attainable

SMART goals have to be realistic and attainable based on your current situation. This is why the emphasis is placed on the short term. If you want to start a restaurant, you might be 1 or 2 years away from your goal. First, you need to get the funding for the restaurant. You'll likely have to work for at least a year before you can obtain the initial funding you need for the rent location, the food supplies, the chefs and the marketing. Goals have to be split into small attainable bits that stack on top of each other.

Pro Tip: Think of goals as laying bricks for a house. You lay one layer of bricks every week, and you repeat for a year. By the end of the year, you have a full house.

Back to our restaurant example: Make it your goal to work overtime for a year until you gather the initial funding. Split that year into goals for every month, and milestones you have to reach every week. Once you have small incremental milestones, you can start taking action right away. The actions will build on each other and in 1 year you'll have achieved your ultimate goal: to own a restaurant. If you just tell yourself "One day I'll get the funding for a restaurant," you will delay your goal indefinitely. If you change your life to optimize for the daily actions that would get you the funding, the mind shift alone will ensure you're successful in the long run.

4) Relevant

Ask yourself: Is this goal true to your heart? Do you want to set goals to impress others, or is this something you've always wanted to do for yourself? Set goals that provide personal fulfillment. You will burn out if you do it to satisfy others. SMART goals are about personal satisfaction because taking action is a lot easier once it's true to your heart.

For example, if you hate your major at university and set a goal to get better grades in school only to impress your parents - you'll likely fail because it's not true to your heart. However, if you make it your goal to switch majors and pursue something that's true to your heart, you will become a lot more eager to pursue your goals. SMART goals are about concrete action, but they're also about flipping your life on its head. If you're unsatisfied with your current situation, it's time to change everything.

5) Timely

Time sets the difference between a goal that gets done and a goal that gets missed! If you have no time-frames, you have no goals. Set specific time-frames and write deadlines for all goals, the most important of which is your start date. Once you have a start date, you know that your old life is about to change. If the goal requires a big life change such as quitting smoking, delay the start date until you feel confident you'll be able to maintain your new behavior. Specify the exact day you wish to start. It's not enough to say, "I'll start next month" or "I'll start in October." The right way is to say "I'll start on the 15th of October." Timing ensures your brain won't be able to think of excuses or procrastinate the date indefinitely. Once the date is written, it's set in stone.

How to Create HARD Goals for Higher Excellence

SMART goals force you to take action; HARD goals force you to change your identity. HARD goals are the ultimate level in goal-setting: They challenge your identity and help you re-shape yourself into the person you always wanted to be. The big distinction between SMART goals and HARD goals is that SMART goals can be broken down into daily goals, weekly goals or other small incremental goals - while HARD goals can only be worked on months or years in advance. HARD goals cut deep into your soul and question whether the action you're taking is true to your identity - and if not, to completely re-shape your identity as a person. Imagine SMART goals as the goals you take action on, and HARD goals as the goals that define you:

- **SMART goal: I want to start a business in 1 year.**
- **HARD goal: I want to be a successful business owner.**

HARD goals relate to who you are as a person: Are you a fitness-oriented person, are you an action-taker, do you aspire to be a doctor/business-owner/family person? HARD goals require deep-level identity change that might take years or even decades to materialize. this is why they're as essential as the SMART goals which we use to power through action-taking processes and momentum-building. HARD goals can re-enforce your identity if you're at a crossroads in life and you have a vision of who you want to become, but lack the directions to get there.

H.A.R.D goals stand for the following:

→ **H-EARTFELT**

→ **A-TTAINBLE**

→ **R-EQUIRED**

→ **D-IFFICULT**

1) Heartfelt

Is your HARD goal one that remains true to your ambitions, values and beliefs as a person? Are you setting your goal to only make money and please other people, or is this something you've always wanted to achieve since you were a kid? If your HARD goal is to start a business, are you doing it to impress your spouse/relatives/friends or is this something you always wanted to do yourself? Ask yourself: What were you born to do? Once you have an answer to that question, you will know if your goal was heartfelt or not. From there, you can start working on your goal or you can completely change your life itinerary.

Defining HARD goals is difficult because it cuts deep in your identity and questions whether the things you're doing are what you should be doing. Often, you will see ties to your past and how you got to where you are in life. Many times, people pursue goals that are not true to who they are, and they struggle because they're going against their nature. Heartfelt goals help you become fulfilled and not just successful. This is the highest level of goal-setting because you question whether the goals relate to your core desires or if you've been misled and taken off course by influences not true to your heart.

2) Attainable

The daily reality of work is different than the imaginary action plan we create. Imagine yourself as a Roman Emperor watching the gladiators battle. It looks easy from the chair, but once you're in the ring, it becomes a completely different ball game. The same applies to goals: the actions you take on a daily basis will be different to what you wrote down. This is why you have to be as realistic as possible, in order to minimize the difference between the goals you've set and the actions you're taking in real life.

For example, if your maximum work day is 10 hours, make sure to prepare your goals for the output a 10-hour day can generate in terms of income and productivity. Many times, our projected goals fall short of our actual daily output. You'll notice that you'll want to do less work, take more breaks, and experience more distractions. This is why you may have to adjust your goals for what you can realistically do based on your historic behavior. Know yourself and your capacity.

If you feel that you're slacking off, you should optimize to improve your performance. Your HARD goals have to be adjacent to your daily SMART goals. For example, if you only exercise 1 hour a day (your SMART goal) you can't expect to become a professional bodybuilder (your HARD goal). However, if you exercise 5-10 hours a day, you can suddenly become a competitive bodybuilder after a year. The small action-steps you take on a daily basis have to be aligned to your HARD goals and big-picture perspective.

3) Required

HARD goals must be critical. They can't be a mere formality. A HARD goal has to be critical to your existence, and you must feel an immediate urge to act on a HARD goal. It has to be tied deep in your core being, or they're not worth pursuing. Ask yourself: What is itching you right now that you're not acting on? Do you have a business idea and see people opening similar businesses that you could do better than them? Is this weighing on your soul deeply? If so, you must take action.

Are you worried that you'll miss out on Bitcoin if you don't invest now? Are you worried someone will take your business idea if you don't do it now? If the HARD goal is time-sensitive and you're feeling a deep urge to act on it right now, this is something you should pursue. If you want to pursue a formality, it's definitely not a HARD goal. For example, moving out of your neighborhood to a better neighborhood is a SMART goal, but is it really a HARD goal that challenges your core identity? It's not. A HARD goal is something that changes who you are, and challenges your currently worldview on what you deem possible.

4) Difficult

If the goals aren't difficult, they're not worth pursuing. If you can get something done without changing your whole life, you must think bigger! Ask yourself: What is the hardest thing you can do right now? The task that will require the most mental energy, the longest hours at work, and the most sacrifice on your end — this is what your HARD goal should be. HARD goals are meant to be difficult and challenge your very being, in order to trigger the change that you want to extract out of life.

Avoid setting medium-difficulty goals such "lose 10 pounds of fat" or "get a promotion at work" — those are SMART goals. The right approach to setting hard goals is to aim for the top. How can you become the fittest you've ever been in your life and reach your genetic potential at the gym? How can you find the highest paying job in your industry and work for the largest corporation? How can you start a profitable corporation and become one of the most successful brands in the world?

This is a difficult task, one that might require 5 or 10 years of perseverance, but that gives your life meaning in the grand scale. A truly difficult task will challenge your existence, make you question your course in life and ultimately allow you to become what you've always dreamed to become.

Exercise: To define your HARD goals, ask yourself the following questions and write the answers down on a piece of paper:

- Where do I want to be in 5 years?
- What do I intend to do about it?
- What am I afraid to miss out on in life?
- What do I plan to do about this?
- What change will that require from me?

The answers to those questions will give you insight in terms of your real, heartfelt long-term goals. Once you have the answers written down, you can cross-reference whether your HARD goals stand for the values listed above.

The Secrets to Turning Your Goals into Achievable Steps

Have you decided on goals you're stuck at the starting point but you don't know where to start? Are you too overwhelmed with the goal-setting process, and are the multiple goals you've set confusing you? Do you have a big "bucket list" to check off and you don't know how to prioritize your goals? Goal-setting can overwhelm a person because they're making too many changes at once. If your work occupies half of your day, and you're tired at the end of the day, how are you supposed to find the energy to exercise?

Let's say you want to start a business but you need $100,000 in inventory to start. Where do you get the investment money? What about bad habits and addictions? if you're trying to quit cigarettes, alcohol and drugs, how do you know when enough is enough? The wrong approach is to try to do everything at once — you will be overwhelmed. You might last for a few weeks, but then your motivation will dip. The right approach is to prioritize your goals, and act on each one individually until your actions are working in conjunction.

Most people lose motivation after 4 weeks. The biggest reason for that is that they set their goals too high and end up overwhelmed. For example, if someone tries to lose 20 pounds in 4 weeks, they might be successful during the first week using a starvation diet, but then they'll go right back to their old eating habits once their hunger kicks back in. The smarter approach for them would be to replace their foods with healthier ones, which will take longer than a starvation diet, but it's consistent.

If you set high expectations, your goal list is going to be full. This can be a negative because if you do too many things at once you will lose track of the meaning of those things. Prioritizing your goals and allocating your action steps gradually is critical. It's better to take on fewer goals that have more meaning to you, than many goals that have lesser meaning.

Goals can be converted to action steps with a simple 4-step process:

1) Don't Aim Too High

If you aim too high, you'll be disappointed if you don't make it. For example, if you aim to make $1 million dollars in 6 months or climb Mount Everest in 1 month, you'll likely fail. Set realistic goals based on your competency. If you're not competent, delay your goal until a point where you'll obtain the competency. If you want to climb Mt Everest, you won't be able to prepare for it in 1 month. However, if you prepare for a year in advance, there is a higher chance you'll be able to climb it given 12 months of practice.

If you want to become a millionaire, set it as a 5-year or a 10-year goal. This way you have enough time to develop and grow your business, or make it high up the corporate ladder. The right approach is to aim for moderate goals that you can achieve by preparing yourself and acting in small increments. If you aim too high, you will burn yourself out. The most effective measurement to prepare for realistic goals is to imagine an easy goal and double it.

Set goals based on evidence from the past. If you've lost 10 pounds in a month once, expect that you'll be able to repeat that. If you've made $100,000 in a year, you should be able to replicate that. In the former, it's wrong to aim for 50 pounds a month or $100,000 in a month instead of a year. Once you have evidence or a pattern you can use to judge your performance, you can plan in advance because your goals will be solidified by past evidence.

2) Limit the Number of Goals

Let's say you have 10 goals on your bucket list: 1) to move to another city 2) to lose 20 pounds 3) to quit smoking 4) to get a better job 5) to stop drinking 6) to travel to India 7) to meet a romantic partner 8) to learn the guitar 9) to wake up at 5 AM 10) to start meditating. Would those goals be realistic in 1 year? The answer is yes, but the sheer amount of goals would overwhelm you. The fact is that when you spread yourself out between dozens of goals, you won't know where to start and you will lose focus on the ones that matter.

Most people write down goals that are completely insignificant to their growth as a person — goals such as learning to play an instrument or waking up earlier. Significant goals are goals that propel you forward by helping you drop dead-weight such as addictions and help you make big moves such as finding a better job or starting a business. Limit the amount of goals you're setting by opting for a maximum of 3 goals a year - those goals should reflect your biggest desires.

3) Sort Goals by Priority

If you hate your body, make it your #1 goal to lose weight. If you're unsatisfied with your monetary situation, focus on finding a new job. If your health is suffering due to an addiction, make it your priority to quit your addiction. To prioritize goals, identify what would trigger the biggest change in your life. For instance, starting a business would make a far bigger difference than learning to play the guitar. Once you've cut down your goals to only 2-3 core goals that matter, you should sort them by your competency level.

Start with the goal that you're the most competent at, because this will build the leverage to proceed onto harder goals. If you have to choose between losing weight, finding a new job and dropping an addiction - start with whichever one you're the most confident you'll succeed at first: If you have previous fitness experience, start with weight loss. If you have experience switching jobs, find a new job first. If your bad habit is not a major part of your life, drop it first.

4) Chop Goals Down in Weekly Increments

Break down your goals in weekly increments, or small milestones that you can cross out weekly. Start by "zooming in" on your larger goal. If you have a goal that will take you 1 year to achieve, set smaller monthly milestones. Once you've set the monthly milestones, set weekly milestones that feed into your larger monthly milestones. This way you can exclusively focus your attention on your weekly output, and that weekly output will translate to gradual monthly output until you've reached your final yearly goal.

The way to be effective with large-scale goals that take a lot of time is to start small. Remember this: **"You are the culmination of your daily actions."** If you set a milestone for each week, and you carry out your tasks on the daily, consider yourself successful. This is because the weeks will compound and you'll eventually obtain your larger goals.

How to Reward Yourself for Progress

What if you're successful for 2 weeks, you take a break and you immediately fall back in old unhealthy habits? What if you quit smoking and go right back after 4 weeks? Are you worried that if you take a break, you'll lose momentum and all your hard work will be for nothing? Many people relapse on their bad habits when they're let off the hook - this is because they've been kept on a leash for weeks or months at a time, and start craving their old lifestyle. It's extremely difficult to change your ways, but to avoid burnout a person has to take some time off and reward themselves regularly. To reward yourself without slipping back into your old habits, it's important to plan out small "rewards" accordingly.

Logistics planning your rewards is the first step. For example, if you quit smoking and you want to celebrate that fact, it's better to book a holiday abroad instead of go to a party. Once you're on a holiday you'll be able to relax on a beach and soak in the fresh air, while a party you would be tempted you to go right back to your smoking habit. If you've changed your diet and you now only consume organic food, you have to be careful not to fall to the temptation of your old unhealthy ways of living.

Why Reward Yourself Now?

Rewarding yourself is useful for two reasons: 1) It reinforces that you're successful and crossed a certain milestone 2) It helps to avoid burnout at work. People who work hard will often times spend days entire locked inside their offices in order to work harder and increase productivity. If they do this for weeks at a time they risk "burnout", and essentially start losing motivation. To avert this process, there are many ways to break the chain by rewarding yourself temporarily; until you're fully recharged and you can go back to your work schedule. If you're celebrating a small milestone, start with a small celebration. If you've achieved big success you should consider taking more time off to reward yourself and maybe even take a whole month off.

Pro Tip: Rewarding yourself is not about posting on social media. Did you lose 5 pounds in a week? Did you stop eating junk food for a week? Did you quit smoking recently? These are worthy of celebration, but a reward has to fulfill you spiritually by showing you a new side of life, one that is not prone to external validation.

The following are the best ways to unwind and reward yourself after achieving a milestone:

1) Book a Weekend Holiday

Book a weekend holiday to a place that looks nothing like your office: The mountain, beach, lake — nature of any kind. Forget about the sound of computers and phones going off, and unplug yourself from modern society. If you've been working for weeks at time, your body is full of a stress chemical called cortisol. To flush it out of your system, you have to change your environment completely. Flights can be cheap and you can book a flight for your break in advance — both cheaper and motivating as you'll expect a reward while you're working.

It's possible to travel on a budget by flying with cheap airlines and staying in cheap housing or even house shares if you're young. Make your destination as different to your current place of work as possible. If you work in a busy place, make your destination a quiet place where you can sit and do nothing. Don't overdo it. Most times, 1-2 days at the beach is enough. Sit by the ocean and listen to the waves at night. Watch the stars. Take time to think about what you did in retrospect, and what future big projects are ahead of you. Try to meditate on your thoughts. This will free you of cortisol and recharge you. You will reward yourself by changing your environment and your brain will reinforce the fact that you're successful.

2) Create a Movie Night

Humans are social creatures. Historically, we evolved to live in 150-person tribes and millions of years of evolution we spent living closely to other people. This made us crave social activity, and engaging with people socially makes us more relaxed. If you're uncomfortable at parties due to high amounts of alcohol, a movie night is the perfect reward for you. Invite your closest friends and family for a movie or a Netflix comedy. Cook some popcorn and spend the night watching movies. If you've achieved a lot of success, you can even drink and order junk for the night. You've earned it. Finish your movie night off by preparing a nice late-night bubble bath with wine. This way you can socialize and relax, and then complete your relaxation with a long relaxing therapy bath.

3) Explore the City

Go out to your city and do the first activity you come across. Watch a football game, go see a tourist attraction, go to a bar, participate in a festival. If you live in a major city where there are activities going on around the clock. Cities are full of entertainment options that can provide you with fun activities around the clock. Do you miss your childhood days when you were carefree and driving go-karts? Go find one and invite your friend. This will make you feel carefree, and you can combine multiple activities at once. How about you see a new blockbuster at the cinema, and top your evening off with a trip to your favorite bar? Your city probably has many hidden attractions and areas that you can explore. If you don't want to spend money, you can just walk and listen to music. Walking is a very meditative activity because it allows you to soak in the energy of the city.

4) Buy Yourself a Gift

Pretend it's your birthday and get yourself something you always wanted but didn't have the courage to purchase because you were conservative with your money. Did you want to get one of the new iPhones for a while, but held off from purchasing them? Reward yourself by buying a new phone. Go to your favorite book store and purchase a new book. Take a trip to the department store and try out a new pair of jeans. Go pick up a new pair of Nikes. Old-school consumerism can relax you. Appeal can make you feel new and refresh your sense of fashion. Whatever you've been missing out on, reward yourself by buying an item that you always wanted.

4 Ways to Create a Goal-Friendly Environment

Do you live in a loud household where you can't get anything done because the noises interrupt you? Are your neighbors noisy and interrupting you constantly while you're trying to get work done? Is your desk cluttered and disorganized and you struggle to organize your belongings? The environment you reside in will have repercussions on your productivity - the same as the people influencing you.

Bruce Lee used to say "If you put water into a cup, it becomes the cup. If you put water into a bottle, it becomes the bottle." In other words, you are a product of your environment. What happens when your environment is sub-par and preventing you from achieving your peak productive potential? It's time to clean house. This can mean organizing your current living space, or it could mean completely replacing your space by moving into a new neighborhood. The physical environment in which you reside in will dictate your energy output. To make the most out of your energy, you have to live in the kind of environment that is organized for productivity.

The following 4 techniques will help you create a goal-friendly environment:

1) Clean Your Room

To become productive, you have to minimize your office space to only the essential tools you need: The desk, chair, computer and/or any other tools necessary for the job. Dump everything else in the trash. If your environment is cluttered with food, boxes from eBay orders, electronics, clothes and other messy things - this will reflect in your productivity because you'll be constantly distracted by everything around you. The same applies for your computer: clear out your desktop and put every distracting icon such as games and music into a separate folder.

Only allow the most critical software on your desktop. If your room is dirty, take a full day to clean it and dispose of any items that aren't critical to your productivity. Give your old clothes away to the Red Cross. Make sure you have freedom to move your hands and that you're sitting in a forward position if you're working at an office. Your back will be exhausted from 10-hour shifts and you must give it adequate support. Once you've removed all unnecessary items and your room is clean, you'll be ready to start producing.

2) Move to a Different Area

Do you live with in an area that is too loud and distracting? If you answered yes, move out. The difference in productivity you'll experience will make up for the loss of living in a rent-free environment. Find a new apartment in a peaceful area where you can focus 100% on your work. This will enable you to minimize all distractions and maximize productivity. Moving out is a radical tactic, as many people sign contracts for rental properties that expire after 6 months or a year. However, the increase in productivity is worth it effort.

Move out even if your interior living situation is ideal but the area is too harmful to your goals. If you live in a central area of the city where bars play loud music at night, this will affect your sleep. Aim to live in an area that is suitable to your goals. For example, if you want to lose weight and you live in an area with many bakeries and fast-food joints, move to a place where there are health food stores and jogging paths. This way, you can exercise and purchase good food instead of being tempted by unhealthy food.

3) Cut Off Bad Influences

If some people such as your love partner or even your parents are holding you back by interrupting your schedule, cut them off. Our habits are formed by the people we surround ourselves with, and if the people closest to you are not aligned with your goals this can create inconvenience for both of you. It's wise to break contact with people temporarily to see if they make a difference. For example, if you're staying in your parent's place to save money but you are made to feel like a nuisance, it's better to move out. Your productivity will increase once you're free to work in your own living space. If you have friends with bad habits who influence you directly or indirectly, cut them off until you drop your bad habits and they can no longer influence you. Sometimes you can end relationships temporarily and re-start them once you've gained ground on your productivity.

4) Go to a Goal-Friendly Environment

Modern society has living spaces and environments that cater to goal-oriented people. The most notable examples include meditation clubs and co-working spaces. Co-working spaces are a relatively new invention for creative people who want to network together while they're working. A person can join a co-working space by purchasing a membership card similar to a gym. This allows them to network with like-minded individuals and focus when they need to work. There are many clubs such as meditation clubs where a person can learn a new skill and organize with individuals who are familiar with the practice. If you can't create a goal-friendly environment, you can join an existing one directly.

Chapter 4 - Techniques to Amp Up Output

Transform Your Life with the Getting Things Done (GTD) Method

Do you forget small things? Have you reminded yourself you need to get something done the whole day and then ended up forgetting about it? One day at work your boss tasks you to bring a business paper to work. You go back home and become paranoid: Your mind thinks, "Get that business paper" while you're eating, your start thinking of business papers when you're petting your dog, you go for a jog thinking about business papers at night, you almost trip on the stairs thinking about business papers, and in bed you lay awake at 3 AM thinking about the business papers.

The next morning, what happens? You get distracted by the news of the conflict in Syria, you see your dog made a mess in the kitchen, your wife starts telling you about unpaid bills — and what is the last thing you think of? The business papers. That's right, you forgot. A very popular technique that helps you remember and organize your life is the GTD method by David Allen.

The "Get Things Done" (GTD) method was invented by productivity consultant David Allen, an expert in productivity consulting with over 30 years of experience. The book became one of the most iconic and best-selling productivity books of all time. The GTD method is a 5-step method that focuses on writing down everything related to the mind, removing the unnecessary, and converting "actionable" and "unactionable" thoughts into appropriate "work tasks."

GTD is not for everyone — this is a system for people who have time to consider everything and wish to take control over their life by re-evaluating their life decisions. Example: Your boss tasks you to bring business papers at work. What is your "reminder" here? It's to bring business papers. The GTD method explains that the "reminder" has to be removed from your head by writing it down. You basically convert it to an "action item" on your big paper. We can effectively convert all planned tasks into action items and organize them down by priority. This shifts our attention from thinking about reminders to do to actually taking actionable steps. The GTD technique focuses on important tasks, so all tasks that require less than 2 minutes to complete shouldn't be written down.

The GTD Technique is a 5-step process:

Step 1: Capture

Step 2: Clarify

Step 3: Organize

Step 4: Reflect

Step 5: Engage

How it works: The GTD technique is based on taking note all your "incompletes" (things you have to do), then deciding if the "incompletes" are 1) "actionable" (ones you take action on) or 2) "unactionable" (ones you can't do anything about) and then taking action by focusing on the most important work items you've written down. The GTD technique requires a complete "brain dump" in order to jot down everything that preoccupies your mind.

Once you've completed your brain dump, you have to split the incompletes in 2 ways: actionable and unactionable. The unactionable incompletes are discarded, while the actionable ones are prioritized based on which one has the highest impact on your life and productivity. The GTD method requires a lot reflection and can't be done in a single sitting. You must be prepared to spend at least a few hours reflecting about things that occupy your mind, writing each thought down and deciding which one would have the most impact on your life.

Step 1 - Capture

The first step of the GTD method is to write down what preoccupies your brain. Effectively we're trying to complete a "brain dump" and writing everything that finds its way to our brain. It doesn't matter if the thoughts are related to work, family, business or the weather. What matters is that if something is on your mind it must to be written down. The thoughts can be of big, small, medium importance. They can be of personal, professional or other nature — write them all down. Get a piece of paper and write down 100% of everything that preoccupies your mind. This process can take a while because the average human has hundreds of thoughts, but we usually spin the same 40-50 thoughts on a daily basis and those should be written down. Write down even items that are not related to your work.

Example: Let's say you have a mole on your face that affects your self-confidence and you want visit a laser mole removal clinic. Write that down. Let's say you plan to travel to India and you've had this on your mind for years. Write that down. Let's say you're about to start a new business and you don't know how to get distributers for your product. Write that down. Dump everything — take your time and don't rush this. Imagine if an Alien species descended from another galaxy and scanned your entire brain – what would they find? Do that for yourself but only write down what's on your mind. Get your thoughts out on a piece of paper.

Step 2 - Clarify

Your brain dump should have at least solid 50 thoughts written down - proceed by sorting them into "actionable" and "unactionable" items. The difference is that for one you can take action and for another you can't do anything. Simply assign an arrow to each thought on the right and classify it as "actionable" or "unactionable." How do you know the difference? If you have a thought about how you got rejected by your high school crush, this is "unactionable" - you can't get a time machine and go back in time. If your thought was about how you need to lose 10 pounds in 3 weeks - this is "actionable." File it under "actionable" and move on.

Once you've assigned a full list of "actionable" and "unactionable" items - discard the unactionable items into the trash. This will leave only the actionable ones on the table - those are actions that you should dedicate your life on. Focus on removing the unactionable items from your head because they hinder your productivity and rob you of your mental energy.

Step 3 - Organize

You're now left with actionable items - items that you can take concrete action on. To proceed, you must sort the actionable items into items that you can achieve in the immediate future and actions that you have to delay over the long-term. This is based on your competency and time necessary to achieve the action steps.

Example: If your actionable item is to open a bookstore, you might have to delay it in favor of daily work that would allow you to save the finances necessary to open the bookstore. Both thoughts are actionable, but one takes requires more time and effort. This is why you have to prioritize your actionable plans based on which one you can do first. You can split these down to daily, weekly, monthly and yearly action-steps. The yearly actions should reflect your long-term goals while your weekly and daily actions should be updated based on the work and projects that come up daily — those are more dynamic.

Step 4 - Reflect

Micro actionable steps will require weekly changes because your weekly life is dynamic. While many large actionable steps are clear-cut and require longer commitment, the ones we handle on a daily basis will change based on circumstance. Let's say you want to save $20,000 in a year — you can't do much about this immediately. However, you can focus on making $500 a week which would ultimately lead you to saving $20,000 in a year.

If you focus on saving $500 a week, there will be daily and weekly tasks you have to accomplish in order to achieve this. For instance, you may need to increase your productivity on the daily and you must write down your actionable steps for the small weekly goals that you set, which ultimately lead to a larger goal. Take each week to review your goals and change them to ensure you remain on the right path.

Step 5 - Engage

The final step and the most crucial one — once you've completed your "brain dump," you've organized your action-steps and you have a weekly plan, all that remains is to take concrete action. Keep a weekly list of action steps that you must take action on. This will clear your brain because it's not affected by things that are unactionable, and you can focus 100% on the actionables that affect your life. Schedule weekly revisions and add new actions as your projects change, but remember to reevaluate and take a step back every 2-3 months in case you have new priorities and occupations. This will ensure that you're always on top of your life and that you're completely organized in the way you go about productivity.

Achieve More with the Pomodoro Technique

Do you burn out at work doing a 30-minute task and end up slacking off on social media? Do you maybe do 2-3 tasks in a single burst of energy and then you've had enough? Do you want to die when your boss focuses you to do multiple things at once, and you can't seem to get even one done? Many people start taking up "focus" pills and end up addicted to prescription drugs.

Even those who work from home struggle with productivity. We've all been there! The second you have to work, suddenly you also have to take a shower, have a cup of coffee, listen to that new song, clean your dirty room - anything to avoid doing the actual work. We really believe that we must do those things, but deep down we know we're procrastinating. If you're a "perfectionist" you will struggle with this even more because you set standards for yourself and it takes you hours to actually start doing something and even then, you end up with minimal output at the end of the day.

How do you get over this? The answer: Split your day into pomodoros with little breaks in between.

The brain has a limited capacity. It can't focus on a single task for an entire day and requires periodical breaks. Unfortunately, most believe that to be successful they have to do an 8-hour stint of non-stop work during the work day. This is reason modern society is addicted to prescription pills that alter our brain chemistry, and even students are taking up Adderall to focus on studies. Since altering your brain chemistry is unhealthy, the right way is to account for the brain's natural desires to relax after focusing, and to plan out a productive day in advance by anticipating the work-break balance. It's entirely possible to create your own schedule that allows you to focus on small tasks for 45 minutes and then take breaks between sessions to avoid burnout. The technique that focuses on becoming productive for a certain amount of time and then following that up with a periodic break is the "Pomodoro Technique."

Pomodoro: 25-Minute Work Sessions to Success

The Pomodoro technique is a famous productivity technique pioneered by Francesco Cirillo, an Italian chef who discovered that by observing his clock for 25 minutes and then taking a break, he was able to cook more and make better meals for his clients at the restaurant. He had a tomato-shaped kitchen timer that he used to work with.

Cirillo broke his sessions down into manageable 25-minute work bursts that he called "pomodoros," following up each burst with a short break (3-5 minutes) for relaxation. He didn't do this the whole day, but once he completed 4 pomodoros, he took a longer 30-minute break.

The Pomodoro Technique is a brain technique that optimizes your brain for work output but then relaxes it to avoid burnout. This follows a natural cycle that responds to our evolutionary nature. When we used to hunt in the wilderness millions of years ago, we would usually find an animal, struggle to kill it and then take a break. We didn't run around with spears 24/7. Our brain has to receive periodic breaks in order to preserve clarity and sanity. Ideally those breaks can be optimized after 25-minute work increments, followed up by 5-minute breaks and a 30-minute break after 4 successful pomodoros.

How Pomodoro Works: An Average Day

The easiest way to imagine an average day on the Pomodoro technique is to break your day down into 4 or 5 full pomodoros (2 hours each) that you scratch off — one full pomodoro takes 2 hours because it's split in 4 25-minute mini pomodoros and breaks. Once you've done 6 full pomodoros, consider your work day successful. 4 full pomodoros correspond to an average 8-hour work day.

For example, start with one mini Pomodoro when you wake up. Take 25 minutes to work, then 5 minutes off, and repeat this 3 more times. This should take you a total of 2 hours. Once you're done, scratch one full pomodoro off your list. Take 30 minutes off, catch some air, listen to a song and do the opposite of what you did — disengage.

When you work you must be 100% engaged with the task for maximum productivity, but once you're on break you want to do the opposite and allow your brain to recover without adding any pressure. Once you've done your first pomodoro and taken a longer 30-minute break, repeat the process 2 or 3 more times before you stop for lunch. You'll effectively have 3-4 full pomodoros completed by lunch time – this is a solid 6 hours of work in the morning. Come lunchtime, take 1 hour off to fully recover. Follow that up by completing 2 more pomodoros - this will optimize your day for at least 8 hours of work. If you wish to work a 10-hour day or even a 15-hour day, you can add 2-3 extra pomodoros to your day.

The 4 Rules of Pomodoro

1. Activities Shouldn't Require More Than 4 Pomodoros

If your activity requires more than 4 pomodoros (that is in essence over 8 hours of work) you should break it down into small actionable steps. For instance, if you have to deliver a PowerPoint presentation with 50 slides and 10 slides take you around 2 hours to complete, you should split that activity into 4 full pomodoros. This way you will complete half of the slides in 2 full pomodoros. You can't sneak in more work on your Pomodoro as this goes against the rules - once the 25 minutes are out, you must take a 5-minute break or a 30-minute break appropriately. All large tasks that require more time than is given should be broken down into small 25-minute pomodoros. Find out how much time your activities require in advance in order to optimize your pomodoros.

2. Pomodoros Must Be Protected From Interruptions

All internal and external interruptions have to be removed for a pomodoro to be considered legitimate. You can't work for 15 minutes and then browse Facebook or talk to a colleague at work. Optimally you should be focused at 100% during your pomodoro and be located in an environment that encourages productivity. Prepare your environment by minimizing clutter, removing unnecessary items and distancing yourself from influences that distract you from work, whether those are the Internet, people or any other distraction. Focus during your pomodoro to protect your productivity.

3. Recaps Count as Work Under Pomodoros

You are allowed to recap and review your work during a pomodoro because this relates directly to your productivity. Example: If you're a chef at a restaurant and you're at the end of your work day, you need to take the time to write down ingredients to shop for the next day, how much you need of x ingredient, how many pastries you need to bake and more. This helps you organize your day. This is also counted under productivity and it can be measured under a single pomodoro. If you recap and review your work, this is also considered work under pomodoro rules.

4. Optimize Pomodoros for Personal Objectives

Optimize your pomodoros to take actions that create value in return. In essence, the only time we get value is when we produce value in return. This means that to make more money and to get promoted at work, you must increase the quality of your output. How do you do that? By focusing all your attention on the little work tasks that enable you to increase your output. Most people spend 30-40% of their work day actually working - the rest is spent dwelling on work, being distracted or doing nothing at all. If you only optimize your work day to work at 80% capacity with the time given, you can double your productivity and increase your revenues by a huge margin.

4 Productive Habits of the Zen-to-Done Method

Do you struggle keeping your day-to-day habits? Do you delay your "productive" habits indefinitely and end up doing half of what you're supposed to be doing? Organizing yourself can be exhausting and confusing because we're overwhelmed by influences from the external world, and it's hard to "tune out" and focus on what's really important. We're bombarded with stimulation on social media that encourages us to go down the route of least resistance and even the opposite is true — productivity habits can clog our mind because there are too many of them and we don't know which one is the best or where to start. The "Zen To Done" Method is the most simplified and minimalistic productivity method that optimizes productivity for 4 basic habits that you do on the daily. This method was developed by Leo Babauta of "Zen Habits" in order to break a day down into step-by-step habits based on individual goals.

The Human Element of Productivity

There is a human element to productivity — we cannot function like robots that work for 30-40 minutes and then shut off consistently. In reality, we constantly experience peaks and dips of productivity, we feel a surge of energy and then we feel a diminishing of energy. Some days we're on top of the world and we can work without stopping and other days we're all out of energy and can't seem to get anything done. The question is: How do we gain consistency? If the human element prevents us from acting the same way every day and popular techniques can't work with consistency - what is the right approach?

The ZTD approach accounts for the human element by focusing on broad behavioral patterns. ZTD focuses on behaviors that can be replicated on a daily basis, irrespective of your mood or energy levels. The ZTD method begins by analyzing your broader plans, effectively mapping out your long-term and short-term goals and then focusing on scheduling action-steps that you can do on a daily basis that produce the results you're after.

The 4 Habits of "Zen To Done" Method

The original Zen To Done method featured 10 habits, but the minimalist ZTD method (which is most popular) is comprised of 4 core habits:

ZTD Habit #1: Collect

The ZTD technique focuses on letting out all ideas in one piece of paper: Making a brain dump by writing down everything that's on your mind. If you have business ideas left to accomplish, write them down. If you have things that you'd like to improve such as your health or bad habits, write down all of them. There shouldn't be any difference between quitting your smoking habit and starting a business — both are action steps you must do and they should be written down. Take out a piece of paper or open a note on your computer and write down all your goals and things you plan to get done this year.

Dedicate one page for your goals and another page for action plans that you will need to obtain those goals. Take your time as the first habit is the most crucial — it might take you hours to remember all the things you've wanted to do and things which bother you on a daily basis. If you're poor and want to take action steps to become wealthy, write that down. If you're out of shape and plan to become fit, write it down. If you're addicted to a substance and want to quit, write that down. Write down everything.

Pro Tip: To find what to write down, go for a walk late at night and let your mind unwind. Play music and let thoughts come into your head naturally. Once you have those thoughts, write them down on your phone. This is better than "forcing" your brain to come up with things to do while you're locked at home.

ZTD Habit #2: Process

Once you've successfully written down everything, it's time to convert your thoughts into daily action steps you can follow up on. Example: If your goal is to lose 20 pounds you will likely have to take multiple actions - you'll have to exercise, replace your nutrition, drink more water, de-stress, etc. To accomplish all those things at once you'll have to write down what you would have to do in an average day. Maybe you have to wake up earlier to exercise in the morning - write that down. Maybe you have to purchase gym equipment and learn how to cook healthy food - write that down. At night, if you plan to run and lift weights at the gym - write that down. In essence you have to write down the new habits that would be required of you each day in order to achieve your long-term goals.

ZTD Habit #3: Plan

Once you've written down your daily action plans and new habits, it's important to revise your action-plans based on the things you've accomplished. What we plan for and what we do in real life is a lot different. For example, we might plan to run for 30 minutes at night but our energy levels dip after 10 minutes when we actually attempt it. This is why we have to optimize to progressively ramp up the exercise by running 5 minutes more every week. This way in 4 weeks we can actually achieve a 30-minute run, once our physical condition improves. The same practice applies to productivity at work - progressively increase your work load and update your action plans based on your performance.

ZTD Habit #4: Do

Once you've planned everything - DO, DO, DO! It all comes down to action. You've removed the clutter from your head, you've written down your goals and now you have to take the actions that produce the results. Start by scheduling when you're going to do a certain action down to the hour. Example: Set your alarm clock to 5 AM and wake up early for your work. Set milestones you want to achieve by mid-day. Update your accomplishments every day and edit your action plans accordingly. Once you're actually engaged with your daily tasks, you become "self-aware" in terms of with how much work you can take on and you can increase your performance progressively in order to ramp up your output.

How to Keep Track of Productivity?

The computer. Write down your daily and weekly to-dos on a list on your computer. This is ideal if you're working from home or rely on your computer for work. You can edit your plans according to the changes in your life. Many times, we need to alter our goals once we hit milestones, and your action plan will require constant editing. The computer is the best place to do this.

Smartphone apps. Find a memo app that allows you to write down your action steps, or one that has daily reminders in case you forget something. Use the alarm clock to remind you when to take a certain action step. If you run at 10 PM each night, set an alarm clock for 9:30 PM. This way, you have 30 minutes to prepare yourself for your run, both physically and mentally.

Using the "Don't Break the Chain" Technique for Consistency

Do you manage to stay on track with a goal and can keep the habit for one month, three months or even half a year but then your output is unsatisfactory? Do you struggle increasing your yearly output and you're stuck at the same salary level for years, when you know what you need to do to increase your earnings? Do you wonder why this happens to you while your acquaintances progress?

The answer is simple: You're not doing enough. Even if you're consistent, chances are you're wasting a day or two every week and you're not maximizing your time for productivity. Consistency is a giant problem for people trying to reinvent themselves. Despite the initial "push," our biology eventually wires us to crave stability. Unless we assume our new habits as part of our identity, we eventually slip back into our old way of living. The bigger problem is when we think we're consistent, but we end up wasting days that we could spend productively. How do we not break the chain? We use every day.

Solution #1: Using Every Day in a Year

Reevaluate your off days: Even if you're killing it at work and you're satisfied with your daily performance, you should still be aware of the time lost. Let's you've kept up your work habit for a year — you've been working on your dream but you still haven't achieved your desired goal. The solution: Work every day in the year. We're given 365 days a year. If you work 5 days a week, you might think you're consistent but zoom out and take a big-picture perspective — you're losing 8 days a month or almost 100 days a year. The lost weekends add up, and once you lose 8-10 days a month due to off-days and holidays, you're robbing yourself of 100+ days you could have spent working and increasing your productivity. That's almost 1/3 of the year wasted.

Solution #2: Work as If You're Being Audited

If you want to boost your productivity on the daily, implement this one trick: Work as if you're being audited. This is a huge mental habit that trains your brain to utilize every minute for productivity. Most people work 2-3 hours in an average 8-hour work day — the rest is spent browsing the internet, talking to colleagues, sitting in the lounge or doing nothing. If your work solely relies on the output — that is, your income is measured based on the product you produce and not the time spent — you must utilize this technique to produce more in the time given.

Example: Take a look at your day. If someone audits your day the same way they audit your finances, what will they discover? Have you spent every minute of your work day working, or were you slacking off on the internet? Did you take breaks that lasted longer than your work sessions? Identify your problem and fix it immediately. If you apply a rigid and thorough auditing on your daily performance, you will discover areas where you need to improve in and double your productivity.

The "Don't Break the Chain" Method

This is a reliable method for not breaking consistency and making use of every day in the year. This method is for the hardest performers who want to make a big change in their life and assume a completely new identity that re-shapes their life and prepares them for the future. The method was popularized by comedian Jerry Seinfeld, one of the biggest names in stand-up comedy and TV. Mr. Seinfeld struggled with consistency as his job commanded him to do perform in front of audiences weekly, and he invented a trick that helped him become productive every day of the year.

How it works: Take a big calendar with each day in the year, and mark the days you've worked with a giant X. You will soon realize that if you take weekends off, almost a quarter of the days each month will be left unmarked. Start marking each day you've spent working and only mark "X" on the dates if you've successfully completed all your tasks for the day. This way you'll feel inclined to increase your productivity on your off-days and prepare yourself for month-to-month consistency. This method is the final elevation in productivity because it's designed for people who want to make every day count and are ready to immerse themselves fully. If you're actively pushing yourself and productivity becomes a routine, you can use the "Don't Break The Chain" method to implement a chain of productivity that will get you what you want out of life: a higher salary, better fitness/health, more business success, and healthy relationships.

4 Science-Backed Hacks for Increased Productivity

University studies and research facilities have carried out studies that relate certain activities to productivity. Exercising, sleeping better, and walking were linked to a significant increase in productivity and the same can impact willpower in significant proportions.

Remember the saying, "What you eat is what you are"? In essence, what we consume and how we treat our bodies reflects in our mental performance. If we supply our body with the right nutrients and physical exercise it craves, it will give us mental clarity and higher performance at work. To start a life-changing process, you must start by optimizing your health and then applying the numerous productivity habits that exist. The following scientific studies prove that certain activities are linked to an increase in productivity:

1. Exercise Improves Productivity

The largest study that correlated exercise to productivity was carried out at Bristol University in the UK. The university took 200 employees and assigned exercise days and no-exercise days the same people. They observed the behavior of each individual on both days and analyzed how their performance. After the tested participants were analyzed, their results were calculated, and this is what the study revealed:

- 21% increase in concentration
- 22% increase in finishing work on time
- 25% higher ability to work without taking breaks
- 41% increase in motivation to work.

Why is exercise linked to productivity? The act of exercise is not a magic pill, but the mind reflects the condition of the body. We evolved to live out in nature and most of us were fit because we had to hunt for food and we spent our days outdoors. If we're fit, we're able to sleep less, concentrate more and we feel motivated to do more. If we're not fit, we experience constant mood swings, lack of motivation/focus and inability to stay consistent at work.

This is why improving your fitness can make a dramatic impact in your output at work. This study determined that exercise in itself increases productivity by almost 25%. Taking into account that the study was carried out on people with little/no prior exercise experience, it is safe to say that people who make fitness a part of their daily schedule will be able to perform mental tasks at 50-100% higher capacity than people who do not exercise at all.

Stanford University carried out a study that proved the benefit of walking for idea-generation. Two research professors analyzed people who were sitting and people who were walking for effects on productivity and idea-generation. The study found that people who practice walking on a daily basis experience a 60% increase in unique responses to stimuli and generate more unique ideas.

2. Sleep Improves Productivity

If you're sleep-deprived, you're likely to perform worse at work and experience low attention retention compared to people who received a full night's sleep. The minimum amount of sleep a person should have is 8 hours a night - this is optimal as it allows us to recharge. Sleep increases performance, boosts alertness and replenishes our energy. There were two notable studies that prove sleep can increase productivity.

The largest study from the American College of Occupational and Environmental Medicine determined that employees at the college who suffered from insomnia were spending thrice as much time on tasks, compared to employees who had a full night's sleep. Employees who suffered from lack of sleep were found to be less motivated to perform tasks, experienced severe lack of focus and had trouble remembering things. Sleep is tied to all mental performance:

Endurance, focus and consistency. If we go without adequate sleep, we are diminishing our performance abilities by a significant margin.

Varn Bexter and Steve Kroll Smith conducted a scientific study in a corporate environment that analyzed the effect on taking power naps. Employees who took power naps at work were more alert at the job tasks and experienced increases in productivity. Employers are now encouraging their workers to take power-naps at work in order to increase their performance.

3. Music Boosts Productivity

Music is tied to increasing positive stimulus in the brain and idea-generation. A study conducted at University of Miami determined that people who listen to music at work tend to generate faster output, better ideas and had a positive mood compared to people who didn't listen to music at work. The appropriate music might vary, as certain songs can be distracting and if you use music to boost your productivity you should be careful in order to pick a record that boosts your mood without distracting you from the job at hand.

4. Green Offices Boost Productivity

Recently a study at the University of Exeter in England analyzed the impact that plants have on employees in the work space. The study was split in two groups: One group worked out of offices without green plants and another worked out of offices furnished with green plants. The study determined that people who work surrounded by plants experience a 15% increase in productivity and reduced stress levels. Humans evolved to live in forests as trees provide us with natural shade. It's no wonder most of us feel at peace when we're surrounded by plants.

Chapter 5 - Planning for Daily Success

6 Morning Routines to Start the Day on Top

Do you feel productivity highs and lows? One day you wake up productive and ready to work, and another you feel sluggish and don't feel like working at all. Ever wonder why the morning is the hardest part of the day to start working? The morning sets the tone for productivity — if you start off productive early in the morning, you'll likely keep up your productivity throughout the day. If you start off feeling lazy, chances are you won't get anything done the whole day.

Mornings are detrimental to success because the first 3 hours in the morning are when mental energy peaks. The first 2-3 hours upon waking up is when we experience peak mental clarity. This is why you must set the tone of your day in the first 3 hours! If you miss out on this short time frame, you will feel decaying mental energy throughout the day and your productivity will amount to zero. Mornings set the tone for what we do throughout the day, while evenings only prepare us for the next day. This begs the question: How do you feel consistently motivated in the morning? The solution to create morning habits that boost productivity. The following habits can double your productivity and can be implemented immediately upon waking up.

1. Wake Up at 5 AM

Waking up early is a ritual that will double or triple your productivity. The time you miss out when you're waking up late or even normal morning hours can be assigned to doing your hardest task that relieve you of the stress for the rest of the day and "rewire" your brain for productivity in the morning. Most people wake up at 8 AM or 9 AM -

some even wake up at 10 AM or the afternoon. To become successful, you must wake up at least 2-3 hours before everyone else. Set your alarm clock to 5 AM or even 4 AM and start working early in the dawn. This routine will give you 2-3 hours ahead of everyone else to get the most important task of the day done.

Remember that the mind is the clearest within the first 3 morning hours upon waking up. If you use the hours before actual work hours, you can get the hardest task of your day done by the time everyone else wakes up. This gives you an edge over everyone else because you're utilizing excess hours to boost your productivity and you can assign those hours to fitness or other mind exercises such as meditation. If you're used to waking up late, this will be a daunting task for you to achieve but the body adjusts to a new habit in as little as 1-2 weeks. Waking up early won't work unless you go to bed early, so push your bed time backwards. If you go to bed at midnight and wake up at 7 AM, go to bed at 10 PM and wake up at 5 AM. This way you'll get your full night's rest and be able to start off in the early morning hours.

2. Drink a Bottle of Water

Water boosts energy to a higher degree than coffee. Most people don't realize the effects water has on energy levels in the body. We're all heard "hydration" keeps us healthy, but we never pay attention to the increase in energy high hydration produces. Our bodies were designed to consume water, and this is why we can go up to 40 days of no food if can still drink water. Without water? You'd only last a week.

Water is the most essential substance for the internal organs, and water can boost the energy levels of a person by a margin of 100%. If you wake up feeling energy less and you opt for coffee, accompany that with a bottle of water. The body is very slow in the morning because it's waking up from sleep, but when you put water into your body it's quickly assigned to the most necessary parts: the blood stream, the skin, the brain, the muscles.

Water accelerates blood flow by accelerating the bloodstream and this gives you an energizing feel. Staying hydrated also gives the skin a fresh look as opposed to a dry morning look. Water is even proven to increase sex drive in the morning by increasing the blood flow to our reproductive organs. The body adjusts to your individual consumption of water: If you drink one large bottle in the morning, you will likely have to go to the bathroom multiple times that day. However, once your body gets acclimated to consuming 3 or 4 large bottles a day, you will feel almost no inclination to flush the water out. Water consumption is a habit, one that invigorates your skin, gives you energy and supplies your internal organs with the nourishment they require.

3. Limit Time on Emails

Admit it: the first thing you did upon waking up is to check your phone for notifications and emails. If you're working in corporate America, your inbox is likely full every day. If you miss one day of emails, you may fall behind on your schedule. This makes you paranoid because you check our emails multiple times a day. Emails are productivity killers because they distract us from our main task of the morning. The emails in the morning make us think we have 20 different tasks to accomplish, but deep down we know which task of the day is the most important that would push us forward. This is why you should limit the time you spend on your emails and only check your inbox once, then go to work immediately.

If you spend more time on your emails, you'll focus on tasks you're supposed to do in the future which will further distract you from your daily goals. Give your emails one glance in the morning to make sure nothing's on fire. If things look casual, don't look at your emails until the evening and focus on work.

4. Don't Eat Breakfast

Contrary to popular belief, breakfast is not the most important meal of the day. In fact, breakfast is the biggest productivity killer for most people throughout the day. Replace your breakfast with a cup of coffee or a bottle of water to allow your body to "activate" internal organs by supplying it with essential hydration. This way the body can activate internally and flush out and debris that was accumulated from your food consumption the day before.

If you start your day by consuming food, you will load your body on items it doesn't need and lower your energy levels because you opted for food instead of water. Almost all breakfast options in the modern world contain high-carbs: bread, pancakes, cereal, bagels, and other variations of heavy breakfasts. This temporarily fills people but then their energy dips mid-day. If you want to kill your energy on purpose, start by eating a heavy breakfast in the morning. By mid-afternoon, you'll start "feeling sleepy" and you'll want to nap on your work day.

Pro Tip: When you feel like sleeping mid-day, this is your nutrition at work. The breakfast you consumed is slowly killing your internal energy and halving your sugar levels. This is why you feel a desire to sleep.

To avoid a steep decline in energy, skip breakfast and replace your breakfast with a large bottle of water and a cup of coffee. This will give you equal energy as consuming breakfast, but your energy levels won't dip mid-day. You also won't feel that fat-belly feeling but your stomach, but it will empty out and prepare you for lunch when you can consume high-nutrition foods. If you absolutely have to eat in the morning, go for a light breakfast such as a banana, apple or some eggs. Avoid all forms of pastry and sugary foods, as those are the biggest energy killers in the morning.

5. Do the Largest Task in the First 3 Hours

When you wake up, you'll know which task you must do that will require the most energy and effort - this is your "main task" of the day. This is the biggest productivity tip for people who struggle getting things done: Get that task done first, and everything else will seem like a breeze. Start working on your main task the minute you wake up. This way, your brain will get the proof it needs that the hardest task is under control, and you'll get it done in a few hours. Try to complete the task within 2-3 hours because those hours are your most prolific in the morning. The first hour upon waking up is the easiest to focus on tasks because your brain has peak mental clarity, and it progressively diminishes over the day. Start your day by doing the hardest task of the day.

Most people start by doing light tasks that don't require a lot of effort. This is a big mistake because they do a sloppy job on the first tasks and then once they "gather the courage" to do the big task they've already ran out of mental energy. The right way to stay on top of your productivity is to wake up and immediately treat work as if you're going to war: Start with the hardest project, then once you've got that off your back focus on smaller, less important projects.

6. Put a Clock in Front of You

If you're struggling starting things and you take a very long time to start a project, put a clock on your desk. Place a clock in the lower-right side of your computer, a clock on your phone or a physical clock — any clock will do. If you're reminded of the time often, you will become aware of how fast it passes and this will inject a "sense of urgency" in you that will prompt you to get things done faster. Placing a clock in front will also allow you to measure how long you take to complete tasks. This way, you can optimize your work to complete tasks faster.

Example: If you work at a call center and you call clients to pitch over the phone, you might find that you're only calling 5 people an hour. If you have a clock near you, this will tempt you to call more and you will end up making more calls and closing more. The more you're aware of time, the more you become aware of how you spend your work day. Developing a sense of urgency will give you the leverage you need to become less hesitant and take more action at work.

4 Evening Routines to End the Day Just Right

You've had a successful day — you completed all your big tasks, you closed new deals, you traveled back and forth to work. What will you do in the evening? The evening is a time to unwind and a time to prepare for the next day to make it successful. The evening is critical for the routines you set in place and forming new habits. This time of the day doesn't have to be a time for relaxation! Instead of lying in bed and watching TV in the evening, you can optimize those hours for exercise and this will improve your fitness which ultimately improves your energy levels throughout the day and making you more productive.

Night hours are ideal for re-shaping your body and mind because you're almost drained of energy, and you the little energy you have left can be assigned to activities that make an impact in your physical and mental shape. What are the best evening routines? Should you meditate, hit the gym, do yoga, prepare for work tomorrow — or do all those at once? The answer is that it depends on your situation. If you're lacking in physical activity, assign all your evening hours to fitness-related activities. If you're lacking in productivity, assign your evening hours to increasing productivity. The following are the best all-around evening routines that will help you complete your day and prepare you for another day of productivity.

1. Set up an Exercise Routine

Exercise is for the evenings, not the mornings. If you believe that you gain energy from exercise, ask yourself: Have you really exercised if you feel MORE energetic after the exercise than before? Exercising is all about draining yourself — you feel a surplus of energy and you release that energy by running, lifting weights and doing exercises that push you to your limits. Exercise stimulates endorphins, boosts blood flow and makes you look great. If you only exercise for 30 days and you've never exercised before, there's a chance you'll look very different. Your jaw will become more chiseled and defined, you'll start losing fat, and you'll feel high energy throughout the day.

If you exercise in the mornings, you'll only kill your energy because the energy that you use for productivity will diminish as it went into your morning exercise. However, if you exercise at night, you will experience the following: 1) You will be able to go "all out" because you don't have to spare any energy 2) You will tire yourself out and fall asleep more easily. If you struggle to fall asleep at night, setting up an exercise routine will tire you out and make you sleep like a baby. If you have high energy all throughout the day, it's logical to end your day by draining yourself of that energy through heavy exercise. The ideal time to exercise is 1-2 hours before you go to bed. If your bed time is at 10 PM, start exercising at 8-9 PM. This way you'll have enough time to carry out your exercise routine, shower, and prepare for bed.

The best night exercises for you are ones that cater to your current abilities and goals. If you want to lose weight fast, you should opt for HIIT — high intensity interval training. This is a method of sprinting at 90-100% capacity by running as fast as possible. The average training routine consists of 10-20 of these sprints with little breaks in-between until you run out of energy.

If you choose a less intense workout, you should aim to start jogging long-distance. Start by doing short 10-minute jogs and then progressively increase your distance every week. If you feel that you're about to faint and you're losing energy - stop. Don't over-stretch yourself on the first few exercises only because you're feeling motivated. Take your time to progressively increase your exercises.

If you want to gain weight, you should consider getting a gym membership for access to heavy equipment. The average gym is stacked with thousands of dollars' worth of technology that is inaccessible to home-gym owners. The fitter you become, the higher your energy levels will be in the office. This in turn will reflect in your productivity because you'll be able to focus for longer hours, your output quality will increase and you will tire less. Fitness also makes us less responsive to heavy weather — if you're feeling cold in the winter months, you'll feel less cold when you're fit. The opposite applies for hot weather - fit people are usually not bothered by extreme heat.

Pro Tip: Stop relying on fitness apps to track your progress. If you rely on technology you will lose touch with your body's nature: you'll think in terms of miles, hours and calories. Forget that! Start exercising and push yourself without technology and you will eventually become familiar with your physical abilities. You will instinctively know how much you can run and push yourself progressively.

2. Meditate for 20 Minutes

Do you feel unable to focus because you're distracted by everything and even when you start, you can't seem to keep your attention on one task for long? The solution is to get out of your head! We're naturally consumed by our thoughts and this gets distracting because while we're supposed to be working, we daydream about events that have no correlation to our work. How do we get out of our own head? The only way to be effective is to become present. If you have no thoughts and you immerse ourselves in the present moment, you can become more productive, more engaged with your work and produce higher-quality output. The practice that teaches the art of presence is meditation. Anyone can start meditating at home for free.

Pro Tip: You only need to assign 15-20 minutes at night to perfect your meditation. You don't have to meditate like a Buddhist Monk 12 hours a day to be successful in meditation.

The art of meditation can be summed up as "not thinking." Being present is about immersing yourself with the present moment. Imagine yourself playing basketball — you focus on shooting the hoops, you enjoy passing the ball, you anticipate fellow players passing you the ball, you're completely immersed with the game. This is what's known as "becoming present."

Do you even feel in the zone when you're out on a Friday night, you're drinking with your buddies and the conversation keeps flowing? This is also being present. People consume alcohol because it allows them to get out of their head and become present. However, the practice can be replicated naturally by teaching yourself to get out of your own way. It's easier than you think: Start by sitting on the floor of your room, preferably somewhere where you won't be distracted by noises and other people. Then, you can engage in your first mediation session.

How it works: Set an alarm clock for 15 or 20 minutes, depending on how long you think you'll last with your eyes closed. Clasp your hands together and close your eyes. Now focus on your breath and stop thinking — don't even think about not thinking, only focus your attention on the breath. Eventually, you'll start feeling a deep relaxation effect. This usually happens once you're 5 minutes in the session. You'll eventually be fully immersed in the present moment, and then the clock will ring. You'll open your eyes slowly, the world will seem like it's surreal and moving slow. This is how you know you've achieved a fully present meditation session. Once you've practiced meditation consistently for a month, you'll naturally evoke your present feeling and you'll become more confident because you'll be stuck in head way less. There are also joint meditation areas and places where you can practice meditation with other people.

3. Take a Cold Shower

Cold showers are the most extreme, but they're for people who want to push their endurance to the maximum and get in touch with their nature. Cold showers can make you stronger, more in touch with your primal nature, push your endurance and experience health benefits. Think about the old days: Humanity has evolved for millions of years and we've only had hot showers for the last hundred years. Yet, we think that hot showers are the default and cold showers are "extreme." The cold shower is how we used to shower for most of humanity's history, and this is why the practice carries numerous benefits.

The main benefits of cold showers are a rush of dopamine, stimulation of fat-burning and an increase blood flow. However, in practice cold showers have certain "invisible" benefits that manifest themselves over the long term. Cold showers shock your system and supply your nervous system with a "wake up call" similar to that of coffee in the morning. The initial shock makes the nervous system crave radical substances less, and it can help you quit chemical addictions such as cigarettes or drugs. Cold showers completely replace the need your body has for external stimulation.

One more major benefit to cold showers is that you don't feel cold in winter, as cold showers make you resilient to cold and you barely feel anything when you're out in the coldest winter months. Certain communities in Russia practice jumping in ice because cold hits their nervous system to the degree that they feel immune to cold in daily life.

Taking a cold shower should be done progressively. You can't just jump in freezing cold water without pacing yourself first. However, you also shouldn't call a shower a "cold shower" if you shower with hot water and only release 5-10 seconds of cold at the end. A cold shower has to last at least 3-5 minutes to be successful. Start by watering your legs and slowly feeling the cold water hitting your skin. You'll feel shivers all over your body because your body is experiencing the cold water. Then spread some cold water among the upper parts of your body and get used to the temperature. After you've acclimated to the cold for a minute or two, you can get under a full shower blast for a couple of seconds. This will be very shocking to you, but if you embrace it you will eventually get used to it.

Pro Tip: Imagine a cold shower like jumping in a lake. The lake has colder water than an ocean, but once you're inside for 2-3 minutes – the water doesn't feel as cold. The same applies to cold showers. Slow step them and picture yourself as if you're in a lake. You'll eventually learn to handle low temperatures.

4. Read a Book Chapter (Offline)

Go to your favorite book store and pick up a book that will help you in real life. This can be a book related to fitness, business, your profession, or anything that relates to your personal growth. Get the paperback version and get off the internet. This way you can fully engage with the book. If the book is not too large, aim to read a full chapter per day. By consuming the right information, you will improve your life and it will add a sense of "completion" once you've read a full chapter each night. This will also help you fall asleep naturally, if you struggle to get a full night's rest. It's better to read paperback editions because most tablets and laptops have light beaming into your eyes. This is harmful, especially if you're reading at night with the lights out.

Eat These 3 Foods for a Productive Brain

Does your head feel foggy and drowsy after you eat breakfast? Do you feel tired in the afternoon and want to pass out on your office chair? Do you find it hard to get out of bed, to work long hours, to exercise or do anything remotely challenging? This is not due to a lack of motivation — this is caused by your brain reacting to nutrition. The brain consumes 20% of all nutrition (calories) that enter the body, which means that the quality of your food directly reflects in the quality of your brain functioning. If you ever wondered why "organic" food is more expensive and mass-produced food cheap, the difference is due to the quality of the nutrients.

Nutrition is not about how shiny your 6-pack abs are: It's about the clarity of your mental state, the consistency of your focus, and the productivity output you leave at the end of each day. Those are all controlled by one single thing: your food intake. If you put the right foods in your body, your brain will register and function at a higher level. It will allow you to work harder, provide longer focus and enable you to do the tasks that you find challenging.

If you eat the right foods, you'll be able to perform at superhuman levels. You'll work 10-hour shifts easily, you'll run more miles without exhausting yourself, you'll think clearly and become more confident. People report that their "brain fog" disappears once they started consuming the right food. There are many foods that affect the brain positively, but the ones listed below make the biggest difference. If you want to immediately boost your performance, to feel higher energy and long-lasting focus — focus on the foods below.

1) Greens: Broccoli, Spinach, Kale

The three kings of green (broccoli, spinach and kale) are the most essential brain foods that make a night and day difference in the way your brain performs. If you had to eat only 3 foods for the rest of your life choose the top 3 greens: broccoli, spinach and kale. These 3 foods alone are better than almost every other food for removing brain fog and establishing mental clarity. Broccoli is arguably the most nutrient-rich food in the world - it contains all the right Omega-3 fatty acids that build and repair brain cells in the fraction of a millisecond, and it even has anti-aging and weight-loss properties. Broccoli's effects on the brain can be felt immediately! Once you consume a full head of broccoli, you'll feel as if a horse kicked you in the head. The effects are so powerful and they clear your brain that no other food comes close.

Pro Tip: Take 2 days to experiment the effects of food on your brain. The first day, consume the greasiest food you can find: Hamburgers, pizza, pasta. The second day, eat broccoli and spinach and mix them together. Observe the effects on your brain and your energy levels 2 hours after you consume each. You'll notice a significant upgrade in mental clarity once you consume broccoli vs. a low-energy drowsy feeling once you consume greasy food. This is why the latter cost more — they are higher quality.

The following happens when you consume greens: You start waking up, your brain starts oozing energy and you achieve maximum brain clarity. This is the effect of high nutrients penetrating your brain and supplying it with the nourishment it needs. Greens are consumed by athletes because they boost strength and endurance on the field. As a result, you can run longer and lift heavier weights if your mental state is clear. Broccoli, spinach and kale have almost identical effects and these are all premium and expensive foods. Ideally you should consume green foods at least once a day. Learn to appreciate the subtle, little flavors in greens if you currently have problems with the taste. If you can't find them due to seasoning, most supermarkets have frozen variations. You can cook them a million different ways and mix them with tasty spices.

2. Nuts and seeds

Nuts are the most nutrient-dense foods for the brain after greens. They are loaded with positive ingredients that enhance our cognitive functions. The most notable in the "nuts" category are cashews and almonds, which provide the highest stimulation for the brain and they are the perfect snack food for uplifting energy and keeping us sharp and focused. Nuts can't be consumed as a main course, but they are very effective as side-foods that which be consumed alongside main meals. Nuts such as cashews and almonds provide the highest density of fats and proteins that serve as the building block for brain muscle.

To strengthen your brain muscles, you should regularly consume nuts. Cashews and almonds are also filled with omega-3 acids and antioxidants that enhance mental clarity. Scientific studies link cashews to improved cognitive function with older age and studies discovered that they can offset old-age diseases such as Alzheimer's which are linked to the cognitive ability. They can work wonders for healthy, young individuals. Make sure not to go overboard on nuts because they are very calorie-dense and they can be fattening if consumed in copious amounts. A handful of nuts is enough for a day.

3. Fish

Fish and fish oil is essential for cognitive ability because fish contains the highest density of Omega-3 acids. Omega-3's are essential repair blocks that the brain uses to formulate brain cells and increase blood flow in the brain area. Fish have the highest density of Omega-3's, making them essential for cognitive ability and productivity. Oily fish take the lead in terms of omega-3 rich fish, in particular canned tuna. Do you ever open a can of tuna and think the oil is bad for you? It's actually oil that your brain craves — it's linked to better cognitive abilities, increase in thinking skill and brain clarity.

Salmon is also an exceptional brain food, albeit a bit more expensive. To boost your brain function, make fish part of your weekly food consumption. You might want to take it a step further and learn how to cook fish instead of relying on canned tuna. Pick up some frozen fish from your supermarket, lay it down in some oil and let it cook for 30-40 minutes. Combine it with tasty lemons or mix it with greens, and enjoy the optimal lunch for brain power.

BONUS: 4. Coffee

Coffee deserves an honorable mention among the top brain ingredients that boosts concentration, productivity and improves our mood. Do you look forward to your morning only for the coffee? Coffee is an acquired taste because it has a bitter flavor, but once a person gets used to the taste, they learn to appreciate coffee and look forward to the bitterness. You feel "alert" when you drink coffee because caffeine has an active ingredient that blocks the brain's chemicals known as "adenosines."

Adenosine chemicals can be released in the morning and during the day as well. This is why coffee is imperative in keeping us alert and productive. One cup of coffee can supply you with an energy boost that lasts until mid-day when you have your lunch. Make sure not to go overboard on coffee — 2 cups a day is enough. Sip a cup of coffee once you've woken up, and delay the second cup until you've accomplished your work tasks and you feel ready to "reward" yourself.

15 Daily Affirmations to Teach Your Brain Self-Discipline

Affirmations are essentially self-talk that we communicate to our subconscious mind in order to demand the willpower we require to achieve our goals. The brain recognizes affirmations as crossing the border between "I want to do something" to "I will do something" — taking concrete action. Affirmations play a significant role in our transformation when set high goals because they can affect our self-belief system and incentivize us to take action. Affirmations can be applied to all areas of life. They are simple statements that you repeat to yourself when you wake up and when you go to bed.

The way to base affirmations is to consider your personal goals (not everyone can apply the same affirmations). One can create affirmations for losing weight, one can create business affirmations, one can create affirmations related to self-confidence. To determine an area where you need affirmations, think about your biggest problem in the moment. Ask yourself: What am I struggling with? Where could I improve in life? The answer to those questions is what you should base your affirmations on.

The #1 Rule of Affirmations

The base rule of affirmations is that affirmations must be positive. An affirmation cannot be negative because the subconscious mind does not recognize negative affirmations — it only recognizes positive affirmations.

✘**Negative affirmation**: I won't delay my workout anymore.

✓**Positive affirmation**: I will start working out tonight.

Affirmations must be positive, and they must be written in the first person. You must always use "I" when you write an affirmation. This registers in your brain as you referring to yourself, and it rewires your psychology for new habits. The ideal amount of affirmations per goal is between 5 or 10 affirmations. Write your affirmations down on a piece of paper and read them in the morning and before you go to sleep. You can come up with 5 affirmations for every goal. Here are some examples of affirmations based on different goals.

Example: 5 Affirmations for Weight Loss

1. I will improve my food habits and eat healthy food.

2. I will drink 3 bottles of water per day.

3. I will exercise every night.

4. I will run sprints every night at 9 PM.

5. I will get a gym membership.

Example: 5 Affirmations for Work

1. I will wake up at 5 AM every morning.

2. I will start working immediately.

3. I will do the hardest task first thing in the morning.

4. I will focus on my work completely.

5. I will work every day without taking days off.

Example: 5 Affirmations for Dating

1. I will get in shape to become more attractive.

2. I will buy better clothes to make a better impression.

3. I will start going out every weekend.

4. I will meet new people and go on dates.

5. I will find my ideal partner.

Rule #2: Must Be About the Present

The affirmations you write must relate to the present moment. You must focus your affirmations on daily actions that you can take as early as tomorrow. If an affirmation is out of your reach or too into the future, discard it. Only focus on affirmations that you relate to your present struggles.

Ask yourself: What can you do now? The answer: You can wake up early, you can eat better, you can exercise, you can meet new people. What can't you do now? You can't start a business overnight. Affirmations exist to help us after we've navigated through our goals and we know the big-picture of where we're headed; affirmations effectively re-shape our mind in order to focus on immediately achievable goals and "push" us towards taking action.

Chapter 6 - Tools for Future Success

5 Exercises to Test and Maintain Powerful Self-Discipline

Do you feel overwhelmed by big tasks that require a lot of willpower? Would you rather start small by accomplishing small tasks that give you the confidence and willpower to move on to large tasks? Willpower has to be built gradually like a muscle. If you have no weight training experience and immediately start benching 100 pounds at the gym, you will put strain on your muscles. Meanwhile benching 100 pounds bars is a piece of cake for someone who's practiced with 20 pounds bars, 50 pounds bars and 100 pounds bars progressively. Why don't you practice progressively too? To work your way up to the highest willpower goals, you must start with small goals and then once you've gained the confidence, attempt to take a swing the big ones.

Warning: **You must start now.** If you delay your big goals endlessly, time will eventually catch up with you and you'll regret not taking action now. Do you look back at things you wanted to do 5 years ago and wish you got started back then for all the years wasted? Now is the best time to start. Let's start by doing some small exercises that you can accomplish on your own. If you do the exercises here, you'll build a baseline for future willpower. You can also create your own exercises: ones that cater to your individual goals.

Pro Tip: Small exercises help set the baseline for willpower. Even a tiny exercise such as washing the dishes can increase your willpower. When we're out of willpower, we feel like doing nothing. Once we shift in gear, our willpower muscle starts growing and we gradually progress onto bigger tasks.

Treat Exercises as Monthly Challenges

Treat the following exercises the way you do challenges: Do you remember popular challenges such as the 30-day no-shave challenge? Each one of these exercises can be repeated on a daily basis and you can form your own challenges to retain the habits. Example: Create a "30-day no-TV challenge" where you challenge yourself to stop watching TV at night once you're back from work and you instead spend your time meditating or reading a book for 30 days.

Exercise #1: No-Sugar Coffee

The first challenge relates to something we all consume in the morning — coffee. You essentially have to drink bitter, sugarless coffee for 30 days. What will you accomplish? It will push you to get out of your comfort taste for 30 days. The sugar added sweetness to your coffee, but now you'll taste real coffee. Train your brain to enjoy the subtle flavors in bitter coffee and consume it slowly. This will teach you that taste is acquired. Eventually you can improve your nutrition by consuming foods that you didn't find tasty, only for their brain benefits such as broccoli and spinach.

Exercise #2: No Social Media

Deactivate your social media for 30 days. This one is tough if you have an extroverted personality. Your Facebook account? Delete it. Your Instagram? Gone. Your dating apps? Discard them all. Spend 30 days interacting with people in real life and only use your phone to make calls. Remove the pings that you get from the notifications panel during the day. What will this accomplish? It will remove your need to check your phone impulsively waiting on your next dopamine hit.

This way you can effectively focus on your work and all your attention will shift to producing better output instead of watching what your buddy Brad streaming his fishing trip in Canada.

Exercise #3: Run Every Day Challenge

Let's say you exhaust yourself every night for 30 days. What will the results be? You could possibly lose between 20 pounds and 60 pounds, depending on how extreme your diet is. Contrary to popular belief, exercise does not impact weight loss as much as dieting and water consumption. The upside of exercise is the physical condition you build up.

Once your 30 days are up, this is what will happen: You will feel more powerful, you will feel increased energy in the morning, you will be able to concentrate more, and you'll refuse to stay locked inside your home at night. This 30-day exercise will build your willpower because right now you're tired and you don't feel like doing anything. In 30 days, you'll naturally crave exercise every day. Remember: It's all about the consistency. You don't have to run every night, but you must come out for the routine – take a walk instead. The part that matters is that you're consistent.

Exercise #4: Clean Your Apartment Every Week

Take one day every week to reevaluate the items in your apartment and consider everything you own. Are those items essential to your productivity or are they hindering it? Is the state of your apartment preventing you from working, exercising, meditating or cooking healthy foods that help you? Stand in the middle of your apartment and look around: Observe everything. Do you really need that Buddhist statue you brought home from your Cambodia trip? Do you really need all those clothes from 5 years ago?

Is there too much clutter in your kitchen? Do you have too many heavy snacks and food that zaps your energy? Put them in the trash. Donate your old clothes to the Red Cross. Sell the electronics and toys. Leave only the things that are necessary for productivity — your essentials such as clothes, laptops and weights. Repeat the same for your desktop computer. Too many times we have distracting icons such as games, movies and other distractions that have no relation to our work. Remove them all. Do a clean-up every week.

Exercise #5: Meditate Every Night

Start meditating every night for 30 nights in a row. You can learn meditation in as little as 5 sit-downs, but 30 meditation nights in a row will make you a master in the practice. Meditation is about invoking the present moment and getting in touch with presence. When you meditate you feel completely at peace and you get out of your head. You think less, and you observe things as they are, not as you process them through your ego. Once you've grown accustomed to the practice, repeat it often until you can naturally invoke the feeling. If you feel that you need to delay your meditation, that's when you need it the most. Remember to take at least 20 minutes a night for the practice and cut off all distractions while you do it.

How to Create Lasting Self-Awareness

If someone told you "Go run 10 miles now" – what would you do? If you were pushed under a cold shower for 5 minutes – would you run out of the shower? Are you fully aware of your capabilities on the mental and physical level? Self-awareness is the act of discovering who you are — your own physical and mental capabilities and limits. We all have a surface-level self-awareness and know what can do approximately. However, you need to practice if you wish to develop high self-awareness and know exactly what you're capable of no matter the task.

We must test our abilities constantly to become fully aware of what we can do and can't do. Let's say you think you can run 10 miles without stopping. When is the last time you attempted to run 10 miles? What if you ran for 5 miles and you gasped for air and couldn't do it? You can't tell until you try — you need to try it out. Once you know what you can do, you can progressively increase your limits. This practice applies to all matters of life! To elevate beyond basic self-awareness, you must push yourself constantly and test your own behavior. There are practices that can help you discover lasting self-awareness.

Self-Awareness Is for Action-Takers

Self-awareness is about knowing what you can do and what you can't do by testing this on the field. This reinforces your ego in a good way because you've already tested what you can accomplish and you feel prepared to tackle your big goals. There is another underlying layer to self-awareness: How your behaviors impact people around you. Once you recognize how your behaviors and productivity are impacting people, you can adjust your output to create more of that desired feeling.

Example: If you're a musician, you can improve people's lives because your music makes them feel better. Once you recognize the kind of songs that impact people in the best way, you can create more songs that emulate that. This is because you've become self-aware. The practice applies in business: Once you learn what your clients like by testing it, you can deliver more of that product. Effectively self-awareness translates to all areas of life. It reveals how we perceive ourselves and how others perceive us.

You can't develop self-awareness by staying at home, so you must go out into the real world and discover who you are by continually taking action. The following practices will help you obtain a high level of self-awareness:

1. Travel to Foreign Countries

Travel to a country as opposite of your culture as possible: as long as the destination is safe, go take a few weeks off and book a hotel. Pack your bags, book the flights, get your visa stamps - go out into the world. When you get to a foreign culture, you will be tested on all levels: Your social skills when you try to communicate with people who barely speak English, your street knowledge when you end up in shady areas by accident and even the general perception of who you are. Foreign people who have no relation to you and see you for the first time will tell you their honest impressions of you. They'll try to guess where you're from, make conversation about your country/accent/fashion and this will let you know how people who are completely foreign perceive you.

In essence, you will develop a deep knowledge of your identity, your origins, the way you live life and how others perceive you. Travel will boost your self-awareness tenfold. You don't have to interact with people who are completely distant to your culture. In fact, any environment that you're not used to will suffice. The way you navigate when you get lost in a foreign country, the way you experience new cultures and the way you interact with people will reinforce your identity to the highest level. If you're still trying to "find yourself," travel is the best way to achieve that. Travel is cheap, as even inter-continental flights are now inexpensive.

2. Engage in Flow-State Activities

Why do you do some things effortlessly while you have to coax yourself into doing work? Compare how little effort it takes you to play a game vs. do a hard task at work. When you play a video game, you don't have to prepare yourself — you know it's easy and go get into the game easily. When you try to do work it's hard and overwhelming, this is why it takes patience for you to engage with that task. In both cases, you enter what's called a "flow state." The difference is that you get in a flow state with a game immediately while at work it takes longer. Imagine you're skiing down a hill. Your speed accelerates as you fly down the snow, and you can't seem to stop. This is what being in a flow state is all about.

The ideal flow-state activity is one that is hard enough to require preparation, but not hard enough that it overwhelms you: think "medium difficulty." Example: Easy difficulty flow states are flow states that you get in instantly — watching movies, playing games, cooking — those require no effort. Hard difficulty flow states are ones that require massive preparation such as launching a new product in front of a crowd or similar life-changing events. What you need are medium-difficulty flow states: Working on a project, jogging at night, sitting down for a meditation session. These "flow state" activities are perfect self-awareness boosters, because they challenge you to get out of your comfort zone continually. This builds up over time and boosts your self-awareness in terms of what you're capable of doing.

3. Do Hard Tasks Every Day

Push yourself to do things you don't want to do on a daily basis — this will maximize yourself awareness. You'll know exactly what you can do, instead of guessing what you can do. Observe your body and what it responds to. Example: You want to eat, sleep, drink coffee, socialize. What don't you want to do? You don't want to work, you don't want to exercise, you don't want to wash the dishes. These are things you should do! The more you engage with tasks you don't want to do, the highest your willpower grows. Listen to your body and do the things you don't want to do.

If you focus on doing things you don't want to do, your brain will start to develop an inclination to do these without resistance. The initial resistance you're feeling when you start doing challenging tasks is a protection mechanism from overwhelming yourself. In order to push through the initial resistance, you must assign all your energy to the tasks that generate the resistance. This way, you will proactively break through your resistance and you will become a lot more competent in your field of work. Do harder tasks progressively – eventually doing hard things will become natural for you.

3 Healthy Habits for Better Concentration

Do you have this "one" task that you know could change your life, but you end up doing the opposite of the task? Do you think about 30 unrelated things when you know you should be focused on the task at hand? Are you easily distracted and is your environment enabling you to get away without working? Lack of concentration is the biggest productivity killer and you must address this to increase your productivity and move your life in the right direction. Concentration is a flow-state activity that requires patience — it can't be achieved instantly.

To be successful in concentration, you must slowly baby-step your way into the work process. We're falsely led to believe that concentrating is about us sitting down and completing our tasks Rambo-style until the whole work day is done. The truth is that the smallest things can impact our concentration: the environment, psychology, nutrition and even our goals (or lack thereof). If we have all those aligned, we can concentrate on a single task. If one of those is missing, we'll fall in the trap and fail to concentrate. We must start by cleaning our environment of items that influence our focus, and then progressively increase our work load until we achieve maximum concentration on any given task. The following habits help you concentrate on a daily basis.

1. Hand-pick Your Influences

Turn around and look at your office: What surrounds you? Are your colleagues productive or are they slacking on social media? Are there too many distractions nearby? What about your nutrition? What are you consuming? Cut off everything that doesn't help you: distractions, people, nutrition, non-work optimized environments – all of it. If you have a PlayStation/Xbox console and this is something you like to play, discard it in the trash. Let's say you have willpower to not play, should you still trash your console? Yes. The thought that you have it nearby will tempt you once you start working and need a break.

If you take cigarette breaks between work tasks, get rid of your cigarettes because they tempt you to think about work breaks. If your colleagues are not productive, stop talking to them. Concentration is not only about your personal output; it's also about the environment that surrounds you. If you live in an environment that is not optimized for productivity, you won't achieve anything. If you live in a productive environment that enables work, you will achieve a lot. Even minor influences such as snacks can affect your concentration. If you have snacks like chips on your desk, remove them because they increase your will to eat and make you less willing to work. Look at all the external influences that surround you and ask yourself if they're helping you or if they're distracting you from your purpose.

2. Disable the Internet

Disable the internet. This will cut off at least 50% of all your distractions. Unless the internet is absolutely imperative to your productivity (i.e. you trade stocks or sell online) completely cut it off during your work day. That's it — shut down the router and disable your phone too. The internet is the biggest concentration-killer because it gives us immediate access to everything. It's also the biggest instant-gratification tool humans have invented in history.

One distraction leads to another. Example: You start looking for medical equipment factories in Germany for your company. Suddenly you're looking up the town where they manufacture the medical equipment. You're then looking at flights to book to Germany and hotels. After that you notice some food in the hotel pictures and you want to try that food. The internet is a slippery slope as it creates one distraction that leads to another. Disable the router and re-enable it once you're done working. You will still have access to your computer, but you'll only focus on the task at hand. If you need the internet to do research for a project, complete the research for the project beforehand and then disable the internet while you do the actual work.

3. Increase Your Hard Tasks Progressively

To maximize concentration, you have to increase your flow-tasks progressively: Start with a hard task one day, and then once you're in the flow complete the easier tasks. The "hard" task will become "moderate" the next week. This way you can do harder and harder tasks by the week. You have to habituate yourself into concentration by tackling more difficult tasks every week. On the small scale, you must do hard tasks first because this will push you into a flow state of mind. On a large scale, you want to baby-step these hard tasks and take on heavier workloads progressively every week.

This applies to other areas of life such as fitness. If you start with 5-mile run, attempt a 10-mile run the next week because you'll have built up the condition. If you attempt a 10-mile run outright, you'll likely fail because you haven't progressed to that level. Increase your "hard" tasks progressively, and start with the most essential ones. Ask yourself: What would really change my life right now? If it's fitness, focus on fitness. If it's making money, focus on your job or a business. Increase the difficulty of your tasks and tackle them accordingly.

3 Unconventional Ways to Master Self-Discipline

Do you have a more "extreme" personality than the average person and wish to test out conventional ways to achieve your goals? Are you unsatisfied with the norm and do you push yourself way above the formalities and capacities of an average person? Some people are "wired" to outperform everyone else, that's why they opt for unconventional ways to increase their productivity and achieve their goals.

Warning: Certain unconventional ways are healthier than others. In theory, an "unconventional" way to increase productivity would be to consume prescription pills. The downside is that those are unhealthy and inconsistent, so your focus only runs as long as you take the pills. If you actually reinvent yourself and you create a new persona that can focus on the tasks, you'll be able to sustain your new habits forever. This guide focuses on unconventional ways that are both healthy and sustainable — ones that everyone can implement to reflect on their life and obtain high levels of self-discipline.

1. Audit Your Time Like the Tax-Man

What does Uncle Sam ask you at the end of each fiscal year? In essence the tax authorities inquire as to how you made your money. Every

April 15th us as Americans have to provide records of salaries we received, bonuses, how we spent our money, what banking institutions we used, etc. The government holds us accountable for every dollar in our bank accounts they want to know the source of our income.

What if the government audited how you spent your day? Would you know where each minute went and how you choose to spend it? What if someone analyzed your average work day? This technique alone could double or triple your productivity. If you "audit" your time the way the government audits your bank account, you will be able to identify where your time leaks and determine where you can increase your output, allowing you to patch up time leaks and optimize your time for productivity.

Put a webcam in your office and record yourself for a day. What would you find out? Were you working the whole day or did you spend half of the time browsing the internet, eating, talking to coworkers and doing nothing? If you're record every minute of your day, you'll shocked at the time you end up wasting doing unproductive things. You may spend 6 hours not working and 2 hours actually working. Most people barely spend 1/3 of their work day actually working.

To increase the quality of your output, to produce more and to waste less time, you should start by auditing your time. Keep records of every hour to see what you've accomplished and how long your breaks lasted. You only have to do this for one day. Call it an "Audit Day" and review how your day went. Once you become aware as to the way your time leaks, you can put that time to use the next day. If you spent half of the time slacking off in different ways, use that time to double your productivity.

2. Picture Your Success

What if you were assigned to become the CEO of a multimillion-dollar enterprise? What if you were the most successful doctor/lawyer/accountant in your state? What would your average day look like then? It certainly wouldn't look the same as your average day now. Think about what would happen if you were put in a high position in your field of work overnight. Now imagine what an average day would look like for you in that position. Would you be required to do more tasks, to wake up earlier, to create bigger projects? What would an average day look like for you?

Once you figure that out, write down the average day of successful you and repeat the steps as if you're successful now. Optimize your current average day to emulate the average day of your successful version. Once you replicate it, you will eventually obtain the same results they have. This is the act of "reverse-engineering" success. It's possible to tell how a person became successful by analyzing their work history and business moves. Everyone starts somewhere, but the difference is where we all end up. What did successful people in your field do to obtain their success? What did they do in the last 10 years? Did they make certain moves that you are too afraid to make? There was always something that pushed them to go beyond the average in their industry. Imagine yourself at the peak of your success and ask yourself: What did it take for you to get there? Repeat that.

3. Force Yourself to Work

When all other options fail, force yourself to do the things you don't want to do! Force is a harsh word, but in many cases it's necessary. Write down the things that you must do to be successful and gradually force yourself into the action-steps that would get you there. Example: Force yourself to wake up at 5 AM. Set the loudest alarm clock possible for 5 AM or set 2 alarm clocks that go off simultaneously. Once you hear the sounds, you will be forced to get out of bed. Every activity that you must do can be forced. Once you force yourself to do it once, your brain will receive the "proof" it needs that this is something you can do and it will become monumentally easier for you to repeat that the next day. If you can't make yourself do things the easy way, force yourself to do them the hard way.

3 Transformative Ways to Push Yourself to the Next Level

Do you feel that you're on the brink of doing something excellent? Are you feeling deep motivation and you can tell you're on the brink of changing your whole life? Maybe you need that slight little "push" that will allow you to go over the edge and make the first move towards a better life. This is how you know you're ready to elevate yourself!

So you're feeling motivated, you have your goals and to-do's written down and you're excited to get started. All you need are a few more tips that give you a better perspective as to how you should go about taking action. These transformative techniques are for the action-taker — the person who acts on their dreams daily and don't dwell too much planning. If you're ready to jump in, start by applying the following transformative techniques:

1. Be Ready, Not Prepared

If you prepare forever, you will never become prepared enough! You will always hold off until you do one imaginary obstacle, then invent another obstacle. Imagine you're ready right now and start doing the things you want right now. Let's say you want to start a restaurant but you're 10 months away from saving the money you need to open a location. Why wait the 10 months? Start by producing the dishes you will have in your restaurant today. Write down creative names for the dishes, create a menu with prices like you'd have in your restaurant and invite your friends for an "experiment" where they act as the customers and you serve them in your restaurant.

If you're trying to get in shape, why wait 3 months or 6 months from now? Even if you're loaded on work, you'll still have 1-2 hours at the end of each night that you can assign to exercise. Addictions are the worst! If you hold off the "quit date" on your addiction, you might find yourself holding it off forever. Switch your mindset from "waiting to be prepared" to "I'm ready right now." You can force yourself to be ready and remove your imaginary obstacles - start now.

2. Aim to Do More, Faster

If you have a task that requires you to do in 10 days, try to do it in 5. Let's say you have a big business pitch to make and it takes you 10 days to do the research, gather the slides, present the products and make the presentation. What if suddenly the deadline was shifted to 5 days? Would you be able to do it? Chances are, you would. Now even if the deadline is not moved and you have 10 days, act as if you have 5 days! This will create a sense of urgency and you'll be able to get your projects done in half the time.

You will be shocked at the speed in which you can tackle your "big" projects once you shorten your deadlines. Most people delay their projects or wait until they only have a few days to the deadline in order to start taking action. If you allocate every day you're given to your work, you'll be able to get things done in half the time. If it takes you 15 minutes to run the track, aim to do it in 7 minutes next time. The less time you have, the more inclined you will be to take action. Even if you have unlimited time, create artificial deadlines and make yourself achieve the tasks within those deadlines.

3. Use the Gun-to-the-Head Technique

Imagine a terrorist came and put a gun to your head and told you, "Get that task done today or I pull the trigger." What would you do? Would you delay your task and browse the internet while you casually talk to your colleagues? Or would you diligently spend every minute working on the project? The "Gun-to-the-Head" technique is to imagine that your life is in danger and that unless you do the task you're going to die. Once our body activates our survival instinct, we go above and beyond to do things that we otherwise deemed impossible.

Imagine someone put a gun to your head and told you to run 10 miles. You would run faster than an Olympic runner. However, if you had the comfort of staying inside and watching movies, running 10 miles would seem like an exhausting task for you. It's all about perspective. Once you run out of options and you're feeling unproductive, simply imagine someone put a gun to your temple and forced you to do what needs to be done. Remember the phrase: "When you have a why, you'll find a how.

Conclusion

This book is your wake-up call. It's the sign you've been waiting for!

You have the techniques. Now, it's high time to put them to use.

STOP HOLDING OUT!

This book sheds light on the biggest problems in daily motivation and self-discipline. To succeed, implement what resonated with you the most. Consume all the information. Try it out. Use this book as a reminder when you forget basic principles, to keep you on track and kick you in the butt when you start slipping.

Do you remember all those times when you told yourself, "I'll do it when I'm ready"? Now is the time — your "one day" has come! You know exactly what you need to do in order to achieve your dreams. If you've held off your purpose in life for an unknown date, if you've held back your energy and hoped for a better time — remember that there is no better time than the present moment to start.

If we leave you with anything, it's to have faith in yourself.

You will have many downturns along your journey. You will experience a lot of upsides too.

Discover who you are, discover where you're headed, and take action.

All humans are flawed, but the techniques here would help us live with our flaws. We hope you've developed a better understanding as to the mysterious ways human nature works and how our biology is wired to function against our interests. We hope you get to know who you are and grow self-awareness through trials and tribulations. Our evolutionary nature and our goals in modern society conflict with each other. To make our evolutionary nature and modern society work, we have to apply a set of techniques that combine the best sides of both.

Use resistance as your compass.

The friction we feel on our path is resistance — the most powerful force of nature. Resistance preserves the status quo: it's a protective mechanism that protects us from stepping into the unknown. Resistance prevents from changing thinking that it's in our best interest. To do anything different, we have to shock our system and push through resistance. Resistance serves as a compass to point us towards the things we should really be doing. If you feel unwilling to work on your goals, feel the resistance in your body. The resistance tells you exactly what to do. Resistance signals that you're preparing for something great, that something is right behind the corner. If you push through it, you will come out a completely different person on the other end. Deep down, you know what that "thing" is.

Don't delay your dreams — start now.

This book covered the most important methods and techniques to help you establish daily self-discipline. Now is the time to convert all you've learned into action.

As a last note, remember this fact: We're all different.

You have to create your own motivation, your own techniques, your own disciplines. You are your own person with your own goals, your own dreams and your own circumstances. You're not forced to implement every technique we teach, and it's not important to do them all at once. It's up to you to figure out what works for you and apply your own spins on the techniques, based on your own individual experiences of operating and goals in life.

Start by doing something — anything. See where life takes you. Your journey in life is different to the journey of 7 billion other humans on the planet. Once you discover what works for you, start doing and aim for the stars.

www.ingramcontent.com/pod-product-compliance
Lightning Source LLC
Chambersburg PA
CBHW031124080526
44587CB00011B/1103